STREAM TREE

Growing Roots of Faith
Through Outdoor Pursuits

JEFF THOMMES

bookVillages

STREAM TREE: Growing Roots of Faith Through Outdoor Pursuits
© 2017 By Jeff Thommes

All rights reserved. No part of this publication may be reproduced in any form without written permission from Book Villages, P.O. Box 64526, Colorado Springs, CO 80962. www.bookvillages.com

BOOK VILLAGES and the BOOK VILLAGES logo are registered trademarks of Book Villages. Absence of ® in connection with marks of Book Villages or other parties does not indicate an absence of registration of those marks.

Cover and interior design by Niddy Griddy Design, Inc.
Cover and interior images © iStock 2016

Unless otherwise identified, Scripture quotations are taken from THE HOLY BIBLE, NEW INTERNATIONAL VERSION®, NIV® Copyright © 1973, 1978, 1984, 2011 by Biblica, Inc.® Used by permission. All rights reserved worldwide. Other versions used include: the NEW AMERICAN STANDARD BIBLE®, Copyright © 1960,1962,1963,1968,1971,1972,1973,1975,1977,1995 by The Lockman Foundation. Used by permission; Holy Bible, New Living Translation, copyright © 1996, 2004, 2015 by Tyndale House Foundation. Used by permission of Tyndale House Publishers Inc., Carol Stream, Illinois 60188. All rights reserved.

Bible text from the Contemporary English Version (CEV) is not to be reproduced in copies or otherwise by any means except as permitted in writing by American Bible Society, 101 North Independence Mall East, FL 8, Philadelphia, PA 19106 -2155 (www.americanbible.org).

LCCN 2016962272
Printed in the United States of America

ISBN 978-1-94429-813-5

1 2 3 4 5 6 7 8 9 10 Printing/Year 21 20 19 18 17

DEDICATION

To all of my fellow *stream tree* outdoorsmen.

CONTENTS

Preface	7
Acknowledgments	11
1 Down the Tracks	13
2 Vest Pocket	23
3 Lumpy Bed	35
4 Lost Lure	47
5 Don't Move!	57
6 Outside the Wake	69
7 Uphill, Both Ways	83
8 Triple Triple	97
9 It's a Buck!	115
10 Tackle Box	129
11 Off Road	141

PREFACE

Blessed is the one who trusts in the Lord, whose confidence is in him. They will be like a tree planted by the water that sends out its roots by the stream. It does not fear when heat comes; its leaves are always green. It has no worries in a year of drought and never fails to bear fruit.
Jeremiah 17:7–8

Most of us spend the bulk of our time in everyday activities—work or school, shuttling kids, doing homework, or otherwise doing what we consider must-do tasks. But within each of us is a desire to do some want-to-do activities. For me, my want-to-do list is largely focused on the outdoors—hunting, fishing, camping, hiking, canoeing, boating. If it includes a rod, paddle, gun, dog, decoy, deer stand, bow and arrow, camouflage, propeller, lure, tent, campfire, backpack, hiking boot, blaze orange, wader, headlamp, or any other outdoor accessory, I want to do it. And I've been fortunate to do a lot of it, usually with family or friends at my side.

Many of these activities have involved pursuing one of God's creatures. With appropriate equipment in hand, I've spent time trying to harvest or catch deer, turkey, ducks, geese, squirrels, rabbits, pheasants, quail, dove, walleye, bass, pike, crappie, or other furred, feathered, or finned critters. Many times when afield, I've had wonderful encounters with wildlife, seen spectacular sunrises or sunsets, or otherwise witnessed God's handiwork. And I generally acknowledge that it is God's creativity, splendor, and attention to the wonderful intricacies that make the world so spectacular.

Over the past few years, I believe God has been leading me through my many outdoor activities with a different or slightly enhanced view of these experiences. Don't get me wrong, I still appreciate the beauty of the sun hitting the colorful feathers of a flushing pheasant or how a sunset over a remote lake in the wilderness can take my breath away. But now I also see how He is connecting my pursuit of the pheasant or trek to the lake to my faith walk. You see, I think God has made me passionate about the outdoors so I can enjoy my time in this life, but I think He wants me to deepen my faith in Him through these adventures at the same time. He wants me to not just throw a lure in the lake to catch a bass, but to understand that fishing is important for more than fish. To not just lay in a field waiting for ducks or geese to get close enough to shoot, but to understand that preparing for that event can also prepare me for life's challenges. And to not just speed around the lake in the boat with the kids on the tube in tow, but to understand that we all need something to hold on to.

As I've continued to spend my morning devotion time reading and rereading the Bible and listening to what

God is saying to me, He's shown me more and more how the outdoor activities He's given me a passion for connect with my walk as a Christian. Ever since I read the verse above many years ago and absorbed it as my life verse, I've been trying to be a "tree by a stream." By trusting in God, my roots have stretched out to the stream. Tough times have come and I have not feared, but I have maintained a sense of contentment and joy. Challenging times have hit me professionally and personally, but I have not worried. And I've tried like crazy to do the right thing, the good thing, the fruit-bearing thing, to make the world better, perhaps just one person at a time.

I'm going to share some of the "connections" between the outdoors and my faith that He's shown me. My hope is that you'll develop or deepen an appreciation for the outdoors, that you'll develop or strengthen your walk with the Lord, and that you'll begin to see your favorite outdoor pursuits in a different light. I hope some of the dots He has connected for me will resonate with you, too. I provide some questions at the conclusion of each chapter to help you relate. My prayer for you as you read this book is that you will join me in pursuing life as a *Stream Tree*.

Jeff Thommes

ACKNOWLEDGMENTS

I'd like to thank the following:

God, for being patient with me and waiting thirty-eight years for me to acknowledge my need for the sacrifice of Your Son, Jesus, and for opening my eyes to the lessons You're teaching me through a language I understand… the outdoors.

Staci, for sustaining our family during my various work and outdoor trips and allowing me to pursue my many outdoor adventures. Coming home to you is still my favorite part of every trip.

Alissa, for always being my princess and saving your best hugs (and duet singing) for your dad.

Rylan, for pushing me to be a better outdoorsman and father as we enjoy our outdoor pursuits together.

Mom and Dad, for instilling a love of and respect for the outdoors in me as a youngster.

And Dan, for being at my side for over twenty years of hunting, fishing, and other outdoor pursuits. There's more to come.

1
DOWN THE TRACKS

My parents were teachers. They were known throughout our small community in central Illinois as good people. We attended a local Presbyterian church. My parents taught Sunday school. Dad was the choir director. Mom was the church secretary. We prayed before meals ("Dear God, thank you for our food and drink. Amen."). We all played in the summer community band (I played the snare drum). Generally speaking, life was uneventful. I did normal boy stuff, like ride my bike all over—in the street, without a helmet. I rarely knew where I was heading for the day and had no cell phone attached to my hip so my parents could find me. I had average grades, I was shorter than most, and although I played in every sport I could, I didn't excel at any of them. We took annual family vacations throughout the country. Two weeks every summer we'd pack up the conversion van with the Coleman stove (fueled by white gas), grab the three-room canvas tent, and head out on our family trip. Of course, we all followed Mom's meticulously planned itinerary. From what I remember, we made it through those trips without incident—to Florida, California, Niagara Falls—all because of Mom's planning.

In the big scheme of things, there is not much going on in central Illinois. There's corn. And soybeans. Then more corn. Folks call it "The Great Agricultural Desert," which makes me laugh because it's so true, back then and now. When you picture a desert, what comes to mind? Sand. Hot sun. Maybe a lizard skittering across the ground, or perhaps a cactus or two. There are various types of deserts, but if you didn't know much about deserts, you may picture something fairly devoid of life, and for the most part, b-o-r-i-n-g. Now, swap out the sand for farmland. Change the hot sun into stormy seasons. Trade the lizard for some deer and blackbirds and you gain some perspective on the natural landscape I "enjoyed" during my formative years.

Our house was on the edge of the town of 850 people we called our community. We had a ranch-style house with a big basement and gigantic yard. The best thing about this house was that it backed up to a set of active railroad tracks. Twice a day or so a freight train would roll by, its horn blaring. For me and my buddies, that was the signal that a bunch of fun was on its way. Of course, "innocent" boys wouldn't think of throwing rocks at the boxcars. But when we did think about it and started throwing those rocks, the clang of a direct hit on the side of a railroad car was deeply satisfying. Sometimes we would put our pennies on the tracks and see what mutations the weight of the cars would bring. But the biggest highlight was that those tracks offered the trail to adventure.

When you're twelve years old and have free roam of a small town, you take what you can get. That meant long walks on the tracks. Usually my friends and I would head out with a quick word to Mom that we're "heading down the tracks." That *always* meant adventure. What animal did the train hit? How far did the carcass fly? Would a train catch up with us so quickly that we'd have to dive to avoid getting sucked under its wheels? Would we see the local woodchuck? Best yet, we would walk the mile or so down the tracks to the woods, creek, and a bridge. Now that's where things got crazy. We'd chase frogs. Swim in the creek. Climb the bridge. Start small (safe) fires just to see if we could. We'd light firecrackers and shoot bottle rockets into the creek. We were being boys—and it was awesome!

The bridge was an old double-arched concrete structure that straddled the main channel of the creek and an old side channel. A few years back, the bridge had been the site of a train derailment during a storm that loosened the soil stabilizing it. The accident tore up the bridge and created huge cracks in the concrete, exposing a spider web of steel rebar that we had no idea was there. Those were going to be our new climbing spots. We'd scale the steep, slick concrete sides like we were Spiderman. Sometimes we'd hang over the edges, daring gravity to send us crashing the twenty feet into the ground or thirty feet into the creek channel below.

The woods had squirrels, lots of them, but not many other critters. Every now and then, cattle would graze through there, giving us chances to be stealthy, avoid being trampled, and trying not to jump into the meadow muffins. There were vines in the woods long enough to climb on and swing like Tarzan, soaring over the creek.

That creek was your standard midwestern farmland creek. There were trees along it, but mostly just a bare-banked nuisance to farmers in the fields. The cows in the woods plodded through the stream, cooled off, and made it their personal swimming spot. But so did we. The creek got deep at the bridge and we'd take a dip in there from time to time. Frogs often lined the banks and minnows were the biggest fish we ever saw in there.

The tracks were our path to adventure and the woods were ours for playing soldiers, explorers, and all of the other imaginative games boys at that age love to play. Scrapes and bruises were expected and worn proudly like a badge of honor. The only real trouble we got into was the winter when I tested the ice (and my courage) in the creek—and it gave way. My friend was along and was able to give me a quick yank out of the water. That was a long walk home with my pants freezing solid as I shuffled along. I didn't know anything about hypothermia at the time, but I knew what frostbite was, and was certain I'd lose my legs by the time I got home. Thankfully my overactive thoughts didn't win that day and a warm bath had me back on track. I still think that's the closest to dying I've ever been. (I came close again with the bleeding ulcer I had when I was thirty-six that put me in the ICU for eight days—but that's a story for another day.)

When I was thirteen, the tracks and woods became a whole new realm to me. Not that they changed. The frequency of the trains didn't pick up. The woods weren't cleared for some development. We didn't see coyotes or bears or anything. Instead that was the time my parents bought me a .22 rifle. Marlin 60. Semiautomatic. With a scope. Held fifteen rounds. Still have that gun.

You put firepower like that in a "trained" thirteen-year-old's hands and watch out. My dad didn't hunt or fish and had never owned a gun. But I wanted one badly (a few of my friends had them), and my parents gave in. Best

Christmas gift *ever*! We put a sling on that thing and all of a sudden, just about everything along those tracks became a target for me. Cans and bottles, I'll hold nothing back in filling you with lead. Critters, you better hide good. We'd carry two-liter bottles down the tracks and fill them with water from the creek. When you can take fifteen shots at a target that big, from any distance you want, and fire as fast as you can pull the trigger—that's a lot of fun. A box of fifty shells was fifty cents. Cheap entertainment. We'd try shooting from the hip. We'd shoot from back as far as possible to take the lid off. We'd drain the bottle from the top down or just hit it in the bottom and see how many shots we could put in it before it drained.

Of course, we did other things that weren't very smart. We'd shoot into the water, just because it looked cool. Even cooler was shooting into the mud banks where the stream met land. We'd make huge holes when we'd hit right on the edge—craters as big as those seen in photos of the moon. We'd shoot things off the tracks (which, of course, are steel and ricochet badly). We'd shoot into the air. We were generally aware of what was beyond our shot. We knew how far the bullets would travel and didn't shoot toward town. We never shot at anyone and we were good at muzzle control. Despite our plans to storm the tracks and fire as fast as we could, we'd do most of our target shooting with the huge slope as our backdrop.

When I was sixteen and much more mature (or so I'm sure I thought), my parents upgraded me to a 12-gauge shotgun. My friends hunted, and I wanted to as well. Mostly squirrels, rabbits, and pheasants back then—light on the pheasants and heavier on the furry small game.

That's also when I met Staci (my wife-to-be). She lived on a farm where we could hunt, so I needed a reason to go there. That's when I transitioned from just hanging around the tracks and started becoming more of an outdoorsman in the more common sense. As my horizons expanded, that sense of adventure grew with them.

My hunting was limited to those small-game critters until I made it to graduate school in southern Illinois. There, I took up bow hunting and started going after ducks and geese. I've been hooked ever since. I've hunted waterfowl in six different states. I've shot deer with bow and rifle and muzzleloader. I enjoy watching the dogs I've trained find pheasants and grouse. I still consider myself a common sportsman when it comes to hunting. Nothing fancy. Most kids never get to experience true hunting. Without a parent or significant adult to expose youth to the wonders of the world outside of their smartphone, game boxes, or social media, most kids find themselves unimpressed by the outdoors. With more and more demands on kids with electronics and social pressures, the number of outdoorsmen is dwindling.

Despite being brought up in the church, I was just a Sunday morning Christian for much of my life. Church was something we had to do when we were younger. The routine stuck with me as I grew older, attending church, and getting our children into Sunday school.

I became familiar with the flow of service, memorized

the necessary elements, and would even track with the sermon once in a while. But I was still just a Sunday morning Christian. My faith didn't follow me beyond the church parking lot, much less all the way to work. Like many other young adults leaving their homes, I hadn't come to own my faith. So, it didn't mean that much to me. It wasn't until much later in my life that God got ahold of me, and stopped me from drifting along in a meaningless religious journey.

What I didn't know up to that point was how much being outdoors would impact my Christian walk. These invigorating activities helped me to sort out all the changes that happened when I became an active follower of Christ. And I thought that maybe connecting these dots for others might help someone else to feel closer to God while also being a part of the great outdoors.

During my morning devotions, God began to show me that in the Christian life, there's relevance, significance, relationship, influence—that is, *a story*—to everything. This revelation showed me how the development of faith can be amplified through doing productive and energizing things outside. This is not some 8-step program on how to become a mature Christian through hunting and fishing. Rather, it's how God showed me the things I enjoy doing fit with my faith walk. And maybe these ideas will open a door for those not following Christ to learn more about Him—or for those walking with Him to deepen their faith. Some who may be tempted to walk away from Him may find a set of things to do outdoors that will be a consistent reminder of God's love for them.

What follows is a series of common-man outdoor adventures. You won't read any stories about facing down a rhino or mounting a wildebeest trophy on my wall. I haven't climbed to the top of Mount Everest or swum the English Channel. I'm just an average outdoorsman. When I'm sharing some of my adventures, you might think, *Hey, I've done more than that.* That's fine by me. I'd love to hear your stories.

But what I can tell you is that this "average outdoorsman" is a fully committed follower of Jesus Christ. I don't just believe in God—I run after Him, seeking His face. I don't spend much time pondering God's will for my life. Instead, I strive to stay in the center of what I know God wants me to do. How do I know if I'm in the center of His will? It's like driving down an old country road. (We had lots of those where I grew up.) When no cars were coming, you could move your vehicle into the middle of the road for a smooth ride. You didn't have to fight the slope of the road, which would pull you toward the ditch. Of course, if a car was coming, you'd move over to your side. There were no lines, mind you, so you had to guess how much room you had on "your side." As the other car approached, you had to focus on not sliding off the asphalt. Getting your passenger side tires off the road meant a rough, gravel-spewing, unsettling moment of terror. During moments like these, it's easy to overcorrect and end up in the ditch. The best approach was to slow down and gently get the tires back on the pavement.

Living our lives in the center of God's will is a lot like this. When I'm in the center, things may move along somewhat smoothly. I'm strongly aware of His protection and blessing. Sure, there may be bumps in the road where God wants to make sure we're paying attention. There are certainly turns and forks in the road too. When I drift off center, though, there's a stronger pull into the ditch and I have to focus on getting back to the middle of the road. If my "tires" happen to slip off the pavement, my life gets loud and reckless. I leave a spray of gravel behind me, impacting those nearest to me. Going "off-road" is not only upsetting for me, but for all my "passengers" too (family and friends). That's when I need to listen to that "still, small voice" and mind the corrections He gives me. During times like these, He reminds me to slow down and gently get my tires back on the pavement—that is, to focus my complete attention on Him.

But what if you're still looking for Him? What if you're not sure where to look? How confident are you that He wants to have a relationship with you? How will you know when you've found Him? Returning the tires to the pavement can be tricky as you respond to these questions. So, let's see if we can get to some of those answers.

Over the remaining chapters, we'll look at the connection to how some of the outdoor activities I've experienced can help anyone to find God and to increase his or her reliance upon Him. There's nothing like ongoing, dynamic relationship with God to keep you excited about life and all the adventures the Lord has planned for you.

For Reflection ...

1. How do you feel about spending time outdoors? What have your experiences been like?

2. Take a minute to reflect on your story. What are the defining moments, experiences, or periods in your upbringing that have developed you into who you are today?

3. Where are you in your faith journey? Is your faith still something you "have to do" or do you consider yourself fortunate to have a genuine relationship with Jesus? Why do you feel this way?

4. Where are you "driving" right now? Why do you think your "car" is in the middle of the road or the tires are in the gravel?

2
VEST POCKET

Southern Illinois is so different from the central part of the state. Steep bluffs, rolling hills, and trees—lots and lots of them. There are wildlife refuges, state parks, and conservation areas. Abundant deer, turkeys, and (at the right time of year) more ducks and geese than you can imagine. I was able to spend four years in that part of the state, two while I finished up my bachelor's degree and two more during graduate school.

There was plenty of public land to hunt, hike, climb, or otherwise just run around in. One such area was about thirty minutes of mostly winding backroads from campus. There was a gravel bar that we'd park on, right off the paved road. The gravel bar was alongside a small-sized creek, funneled through an aluminum culvert that ran under the paved road. The culvert focused the water flow for that narrow stretch. During the summer, when the water was warm, carp could be found resting in the shade of the under-road passage. From time to time, I'd lie lengthwise along a portion of the culvert that extended from the road into the water and watch the carp. On occasion, I'd move slowly and get my hands underneath the fish as they'd ease out into the sun, then let the current ease them back into the shade. If done carefully, I could rub the fish bellies. The fish probably thought they were just close to the bottom! There were so many fish in that little area that they must have been bumping into each other. On one occasion, I put my hand gently around one of the fish as it eased out into the sun, it slid through my hand to a point where I was wrapped around the narrow part of the fish near the tail. I squeezed and caught the fish. I lifted it out of water and proudly displayed my skill, then returned the fish to stream. I repeated this a few times, just because I could!

Morel mushrooms grew in this area. The tops of them look like porous sponges. They're safe for consumption. We'd go out there and wander the slopes in the spring, gathering as many as we could find into plastic grocery bags. We'd come out of there with our bags half-filled, then rush home to enjoy our bounty. We always prepared them the same way: heat some butter in a skillet and sauté until lightly browned. Serve them with just about anything or simply eat alone as an appetizer. Delicious.

Many of the trees covering the rolling terrain in this area were oaks. I can still picture the forest and smell the fall in the oak woods. These woods were remarkably open. Large trees scattered uniformly and without shrubs or other understory to impede the walk or views. The dense canopy formed by the oak trees halted the light from reaching the forest floor, preventing any understory from being able to grow.

Oak trees, or more specifically, their acorns, are such an important food source to a variety of animals. Deer and turkey love them. When they appear in flooded areas, mallards and wood ducks will feast on them. And what squirrel would ever turn down an acorn meal?

Squirrels will spend the entire summer and fall finding

and storing as many acorns as they can, preparing for the winter when other food is scarce. You don't have to spend too much time around an area with squirrels to watch them take that food source, find an abstract location, dig a shallow hole, and bury those nuggets. Then, come winter, the squirrel will go back to where they hid those morsels, dig them up, and enjoy them.

In the fall, when leaves are beginning to dry up and descend off the trees, the squirrels can make quite the racket. If two get chasing each other, you'd think a small army was coming through the woods. Those early fall squirrels enticed me and a handful of friends to the woods one day. Squirrel, when pan-fried or shredded and mixed with barbeque sauce, can be quite tasty. We wanted to gather a few for just that purpose.

It was midafternoon when we set out. Like many animals, squirrels are most active when the sun comes up and as it sets in the evening. (Biology nerds call this habit *crepuscular*.) We hoped to find a few out early, then more as the afternoon turned into evening. Squirrel hunting can be done with either a small-caliber rifle, most commonly a .22 or a shotgun. The trees in this area often approached one hundred feet tall, a challenging distance for a .22, so we were all packing shotguns. I had my trusty Mossberg 500 12-gauge along. Why a 12-gauge for a little ol' squirrel? Well, it was the only shotgun I had. Try hitting a running squirrel that high up in the trees with a .22 and you won't eat much. (And it's not too safe, either.) With that shotgun loaded with low brass (light load) 6 shot, I was more than ready.

We parked along the paved road, south from the

creek crossing with the "carp culvert," and set off into the woods. The telltale noises the squirrels made by hopping through the freshly fallen leaves, jumping from branch to branch, and dropping acorns from high up in the tree were ten times louder with the four of us walking through the woods. Moving quietly through a forest of dry leaves that sound like Corn Flakes was not easy. The key is to slow down. Every step is placed carefully. Heel-toe—*pause*—heel-toe—*pause*—heel-toe. When we'd hear a squirrel, we'd figure out which direction we thought it was and head that way, still trying to move slowly. We'd try to move when we thought the squirrel was moving (to help mask our noise). We'd usually get close enough to see it, at which time it would see us and run up the nearest tree, running through the tops of the trees to get away.

Now this is when the advantage of the shotgun came in. As I mentioned earlier, a squirrel running through the tops of even eighty-foot-tall trees is a nearly impossible shot with a .22 rifle. But with a shotgun, just get a decent bead on it and pull the trigger. Most of the time, the squirrel would come tumbling down. We'd throw it in the back of our game vest, give the woods a few minutes to quiet down again, and away we'd go looking for the next one.

We'd all done well as the shadows got longer in the woods. Everyone had at least one squirrel in their vest and several of us had a fuller load. We were spaced out a little ways the whole time we were out there, but generally stayed close enough to see each other. There were times throughout the afternoon when we'd have to stop and shout to make sure we each knew where the other person was. Occasionally we'd come together for a water break and quick chat. As dusk was quickly turning into dark, we unloaded our shotguns and began the walk back.

We didn't have a leader. We just followed whoever happened to be in the front. We were feeling good about the hunt and enjoying the camaraderie. As the woods darkened, the conversation centered on which direction we actually were going, and whether or not we were actually heading toward the car. Each person had an idea of where we should be going and when the opinions of two people matched, we'd head that way. We'd gone over enough different, but similar-looking hills to be fairly spun around. Then we hit that point when we admitted that none of us knew the way back to the car. We didn't know which way to go. In moments of brilliance, one of us would think we knew, but we didn't. We were lost! That's about as lost as I think I've ever been. No one likes it and I know why. "Lost" is no fun.

Have you ever been lost? It's a helpless feeling. You think you know where you're going. You think, *It has to be this way ... surely we'll see the road just over this next hill. I think I saw that tree earlier, so we came this way.* But it's dark now and everything looks different. There is no point of reference beyond the few feet in front of you lit up by the rising moon. Without a leader—someone who knows the way and can guide you, someone you can follow with confidence, someone who can lead you to safety—things get difficult.

Professionals who search for missing people say that when you're lost, it's best just to stay put. By moving when you don't know the way, you could actually be getting farther away from where you need to be. By staying in your current location, the person you told where you were going will be able to direct the search and rescue crews to you. (You did tell someone where you were going, right?)

Let's face it, it's always best just to know where you're going and either have some way of navigating or know the lay of the land. I like to keep a compass with me as that way of navigating. Even if I know where I'm going and know the lay of the land, the compass is always the tool that gets me home.

A compass is simply an instrument used for showing direction, with a magnetic needle swinging freely on a pivot, and always pointing to magnetic north.

Depending on your compass, it may allow you to head in one of the cardinal directions (north, east, south, west) or to a specific bearing (north is 0 degrees, east is 90, south is 180, and west is 270). The arrow always points north, so if I'm facing north and I want to go east, I should turn to my right, and when I look at my compass, the arrow should be pointing to my left as I move perpendicular to the arrow direction. Think about it as the face on a clock with north at 12 o'clock, east at 3, south at 6, and west at 9. The arrow always points toward 12 (or 0 degrees) and if I want to head east, I'll head in the direction of the 3 (90 degrees).

Seems simple enough. But in many parts of the world there is as much as 25 degrees difference between true north and magnetic north. What? There are two norths?

Yep! All of a sudden, perhaps those who thought they knew how to use a compass might be wondering if they really do. Using the clock analogy again, true north is 12 o'clock. However, the magnets in the earth in certain locations can cause the arrow to point to magnetic north, which as mentioned above, can be up to 25 degrees off of true north. On the clock, 25 degrees means you're aiming at 10:30 or 1:30 instead of at 12:00. It doesn't take traveling very long toward the wrong "north" before you're way off target.

Because of this difference you must adjust the dial of your compass so that the magnetic needle points to true north. If you don't make this adjustment to calibrate your compass, it will not point you in the direction you want to travel. It's important for your compass to be properly adjusted for the disagreement between magnetic and true north.

Adjusting your compass to account for true north addresses *declination*. The underlying concept is that for a declination of 10° west, the red arrow on the cylinder must lie 10° east of 0°/North on the bezel. Basically, in this case, you are permanently adding 10° to your future bearings to compensate for the -10° declination. If your declination was 10° east you would rotate the baseplate's orienting arrow 10° west of 0°/N to compensate for the +10° declination. In this sense, it can be said that the compass has been adjusted to indicate true north instead of magnetic north. Most compasses that are a step up from the ball/bubble kind allow for this. Try it sometime and get used to checking declination when you travel somewhere (it's easy enough to track down on the Internet).

Many people are aware that a compass is used for pointing you in a certain direction in the natural realm. What many do not understand is that we also need a "spiritual compass" to help us navigate in the spiritual realm. That spiritual compass leads us through life.

The Bible tells us in Judges 17:6 and again in 21:25 that the Israelites, who had just crossed the Jordan River and were moving through the Promised Land, did "as they saw fit" because they had no king. They had no leader, no spiritual direction, no compass, and so they did as they wanted. Don't we do the same? Don't we seem to put our own interests first, concerned about getting and doing what we want? Lacking a focus for our lives that is bigger than only our interests leads to confusion and destruction, just like it did for the Israelites. But to know which direction to go, to have a spiritual compass, we need to draw closer to God and His Word. Our "spiritual true north" is the Word of God. It points us to Jesus. He is our destination. He is where our focus must be.

The Bible is the only legitimate source of direction for life. The Bible tells us who God is and who we are. It gives commands for Christian living. It stipulates guides for good relationships. It provides assurance in times of doubt.

However, there are many things around us that can produce a "spiritual magnetic north" affecting the accuracy of our spiritual compass. Our intellect, unhealthy desires, skewed reasoning powers, along with the worldly pressures, are the "spiritual magnetic north" which can lead us away from our intended destination. Remember that the magnetic north is the force that pulls the directional arrow away from true north.

It sure would be handy if we could just adjust for the spiritual magnetic north by turning our dial. Maybe wrinkling our nose at the sins of others can fix it. Or what about going to church most Sundays? I can correct my compass by serving occasionally at the homeless shelter, right? All seems logical, but in reality, that stuff is only effective when we've already corrected our spiritual declination. To do that, we must stay in the Word of God. Bible study is not merely an optional activity for super-spiritual people with extra time on their hands. It is the obligation and delight of every believer.

We must believe the Bible is true and that it is the same yesterday, today, and forever. It is essential that we accept the entire Bible as true or else we must throw out the entire Scriptures. We cannot pick and choose which parts we want to believe or accept.

Jesus told us it was necessary for Him to go (to ascend into heaven), but that He would send a comforter, the Holy Spirit. The Holy Spirit, who dwells inside every believer, is our Teacher who will lead us into all truth (John 16:13). It is only as we hear and obey the Holy Spirit through the Word of God that our spiritual compass is properly adjusted.

While reading the Bible is critical, we must not overlook spending time in prayer in the presence of the Lord. In these activities we begin to know Jesus, not only as Savior but also as our friend, counselor, and King. Our thoughts will be renewed, giving us the mind of Christ. As we read, pray, and spend time with Jesus, we will begin to think and act according to the image of God we were created to be.

Staying in the Word of God and in prayer, along with spending time in the presence of the Lord, will also help us guard against the influences affecting the accuracy of our spiritual compass.

How then, does someone find out how to use their spiritual compass? What is he or she supposed to do in the twists and turns of life?

First, do what you know the Bible commands. If you already believe it's true, just do what it says.

Second, trust in the faithfulness of God to show you. The Bible isn't going to tell you the name of the person you should marry, or which city you should take a job in—but it will guide your principles in such a way that you will "feel" the answer as God directs your steps and opens your eyes.

If you are walking in fellowship with God, and acting according to the principles recorded in His Word, making the other big decisions will become far less complicated.

Have you allowed God's Word to be your compass?

Are you committed to God and His ways? Whose direction are you going in, God's or your own? Now is the time to be sure God is your spiritual compass—and that you are following where that instrument leads.

My friends and I wandered around in those squirrel woods in southern Illinois for over an hour before I remembered that I had a compass in my vest. This was in the days before GPS was available (or if it was available, it was too expensive for us), so the compass was going to have to work. I remembered that we drove down the road heading south, and that we had gone into the woods on the right hand side of the road, facing down the road. That meant we went west. We hadn't crossed back over the road during our wanderings, and we knew the road continued south beyond where we had parked.

So I put the arrow to my left, pointing toward the north, and we headed east. Within about thirty minutes, we came to the road. We all suspected we had been trending south during our hunting time, because we never crossed the creek that we knew was north of us. So when we got to the road, we started walking north. Ten minutes later, the guns were cased in the trunk of the car, the local country music channel was blaring on the radio, and we were heading home. I think those squirrels tasted a little better than the others we had before. You can bet that after that experience, every hunting jacket, vest, and backpack I use for outdoor activities always has a compass in one of the pockets.

For Reflection …

1. What were your growing-up years like? What are some of the things you remember doing as a kid?

2. Have you ever been lost (or lost someone)? How did you feel when you realized you weren't sure where you were?

3. If you were to get lost in the outdoors today, what would your plan be to find your way back or to be found?

4. Do you know where you are in life right now and what direction you're heading? If so, how? If not, how are you navigating life?

3
LUMPY BED

When we were lost in the woods of southern Illinois, before we could find a way out, we had to own up to the fact that we were lost. If we hadn't admitted that we didn't know where we were going, I would have never thought about my compass. We would have just kept wandering around.

We also need to acknowledge that we are sinners before we understand our need for the sacrifice of Jesus on the cross. The Bible leaves no question that we need Him. Romans 3:23 states that "for all have sinned and fall short of the glory of God." Not *most* people. Not only the *bad* people. It doesn't reference only violations of the Ten Commandments as the sins that folks need to worry about. It says that "*all* have sinned." That means you and me. Despite how good we think we are, or how well we do compared to others (*never a healthy thing to do, by the way*), we all sin. If you didn't believe that already, I'm sorry to serve you that slice of humble pie. The good news, though, is that not only have your sins been accounted for (John 3:16), but also that you can change. You can take steps to get away from your sinning ways—never completely, perhaps, but you can live toward that goal.

In Minnesota, up until 2013, you could put your name in with up to three other folks to have a chance at a once-in-a-lifetime moose hunting license. We had lived in Minnesota about five years when my friend Dan, who was working in northern Minnesota, suggested that my brother-in-law Scott and I, and then he and another friend (in these teams of two) put in for moose tags in the lottery. We figured that if one of the groups were drawn, the other two guys could at least come along and fish and grouse hunt while the moose hunters were out every day. We thought that we'd better start putting those entries in if we ever wanted to get drawn. There were only a limited number of licenses with a bunch of folks chasing those tags every year. We had done some research on past moose hunt success rates to determine which areas seemed most successful. We began discussing whether we wanted to hunt somewhere more accessible with a higher chance of killing a moose, or if we wanted to head into the Boundary Waters Canoe Area (BWCA) Wilderness to try our luck. The decision wasn't so much about actually harvesting a moose, but more about making the most of our once-in-a-lifetime hunt. We decided on the BWCA.

As luck would have it, in the second year of trying, Scott and I were drawn. We attended the mandatory "moose class" put on by the Minnesota Department of Natural Resources, found some guns to borrow (we didn't have our own rifles then), and started our gear lists. Moose season was the first two weeks of October and we were ready to put in our time to maximize our chances. We cleared our schedules and planned to stay in the area about eleven days.

We went in on a Friday, even though the season opened Saturday, to get our campsite set up and be ready first thing on opening morning. First stop was an island on Isabella Lake. It wasn't necessarily an easy paddle out to the island, although it was short. You see, carrying enough gear to be "comfortable" for eleven days in the BWCA, and having the right equipment for lugging out a moose, isn't a small undertaking. There are extra tarps, a come-along, extra packs for the meat, extra food, fishing gear, other hunting gear (for the other guys), and clothes for layering, depending on temperature. Pack all of that stuff into two canoes, and we were riding way low in the water. We didn't dare lean one way or the other when you only have a couple inches of freeboard (that is, space out of the water).

We made it to the island. It was a nice spot—a couple flat-ish spots for tent pads, a decent grate over the fire, some tree cover, and a nice rock outcrop that went up to the lake's edge. We went about setting up camp. Everyone pitched in and did whatever needed to be done. Tents were set up, sleeping bags laid out, tarps strung, firewood gathered and split, and food stored. We were settling in for the long haul.

Camping is one of my favorite things to do. Now, when I say *camping*, I mean in a tent, not some fifth-wheel fancy trailer with air conditioning, running water, a kitchen, and a bed. I'm talking about nothing between you and whatever may come your way except for a skinny piece of nylon or netting, covered by another piece of nylon that is waterproof in case the rain comes in. There's something about hearing the sounds of the lake and woods as you drift off at night that keeps me going back.

Over the years, I've upgraded tents a couple of times. As a family, we can still fit into a four-person tent—although note that when the marketing copy says "four-person" on the box, they mean four very small people. Consider the number they give you and divide by two for how many people will fit comfortably. But now we have a tent for eight to ten people, which allows us to spread out quite a bit when we can find tent pads large enough. I also have a nice three-person tent for my annual trips into the BWCA. It fits me and all of my gear comfortably. Back during the moose hunting trip, Scott and I were using our four-person tent. It worked well for the two of us and our stuff. We didn't have much room to stretch out, but that was okay.

Another thing that I've upgraded over the years is sleeping pads. Not sleeping *bags*. I was good with the rectangle-shaped versions we've had for a while. But sleeping pads, the things that go under the sleeping bag to provide some cushioning between you and the ground, have become more critical to me as I've grown older. The self-inflating version I have now does quite nicely at giving my bones a little extra protection from the ground. But I've found that over a few nights in the same place, what first seemed like a good flat spot for my sleeping pad/bag, can begin to have some uncomfortable bumps and lumps that make sleeping more difficult. As the nights wear on, I wonder how I missed those bumps in the ground when setting up the tent.

Let me back up a step here. When you arrive at a campsite where you're going to be setting up a tent, the first thing you do is find a relatively level spot. You don't want to sleep on an incline. It's not good, whether your head is on the uphill side or if you're sleeping sideways across the hill, inclines are just not generally good for tents.

After you find a level spot, the next task is to remove the little stones and sticks. Why? You don't want those things poking holes in the bottom of your tent (or tarp if you put one of those down first). Perhaps more importantly, they're uncomfortable, especially when you sleep. Maybe if they were small enough, you wouldn't notice them—even so, move the rocks and sticks you can, just to create the smoothest possible sleeping surface.

Sometimes you miss some rocks and sticks and you have to reach under the tent, or even move the tent, for a brief period to get them out. Sometimes, there are bigger rocks or roots that you don't see at first, but begin to feel as the nights wear on. A big root. A rock that was barely sticking out of the ground. Those don't come out easy. You didn't even realize they were there, but getting them out is going to be tough. You need to dig and dig or chop and chop to get them out. You can't leave them there. Once you know they're there, they become the only thing you notice when you lie down, and they may keep you from getting the rest you need. You may sleep, but I guarantee that those sticks, stones, roots, or large rocks that you don't move will rob you of any real rest. Without that rest, you won't be able to maximize your effectiveness the next day. If you're camping, chances are that you're doing something the next day in which you need all the energy you can get.

Bad habits and sins are the same as those rocks and roots. When we first become Christians, God points out some attitudes and behaviors in our character that are easy to see and need clearing out. We can get rid of the ones on the surface easily. Like picking up stones and sticks before laying out our tent. But what about the big rocks and roots? Those are the ones that others don't see as often that continue to make you uncomfortable. You may not even realize it at first.

Do you have a bad habit you'd like to overcome? A bad habit is usually connected to wrong beliefs and attitudes. We should not want to change a habit only because it is embarrassing, expensive, unhealthy, or makes us feel guilty—rather we should want God's greater purpose for our life to be fulfilled. Until we deal with the underlying wrong beliefs that weaken our resistance to the bad habit, we will have only limited success in overcoming it.

We must see that bad habits are ultimately spiritual issues. When appropriate, we must not hesitate to call them *sins*. We need to realize that the means of *sanctification* (to be made holy) described in Scripture is essential for overcoming such habits.

It is critical that we internalize responsibility for our

own sins. We must own up to our own harmful habits and again, not shrink from calling them sin. As I mentioned before, Romans 3:23 states that "for all have sinned and fall short of the glory of God."

The good news is that sinful habits are not insurmountable problems for the Christian. After all, the Holy Spirit dwells within us and is working to conform us to the image of Christ. "And if God is for us, who can be against us?" (Romans 8:31). Galatians 5:16 says that if we "walk by the Spirit, and [we] will not carry out the desire of the flesh" (NASB). First Corinthians 10:13 is a promise that God will not permit us to be tempted beyond our ability in that "no temptation has overtaken you except what is common to mankind. And God is faithful; he will not let you be tempted beyond what you can bear. But when you are tempted, he will also provide a way out so that you can endure it." If we make use of the resources provided by God through His Spirit and His Word, we can attack any habit knowing that we can overcome it, by the grace and power of God.

There's another way for overcoming a bad habit. Remember that sin begins in the mind. James 1:14–15 compares a person falling into sin to a fish or animal that is caught with bait: "But each person is tempted when they are dragged away by their own evil desire and enticed. Then, after desire has conceived, it gives birth to sin; and sin, when it is full-grown, gives birth to death." It sees the bait, desires it, and is trapped in the process of grabbing it. Likewise, sins that ensnare us begin in the mind.

The person who steals first thinks about the thing he wants. He then thinks of a plan for getting it. After he has schemed in his mind, he takes it. He could have stopped the sin in his mind before it became completed in his action. That's why Scripture commands us to renew our minds, as described in Romans 12:2, "Do not conform to the pattern of this world, but be transformed by the renewing of your mind. Then you will be able to test and approve what God's will is—his good, pleasing and perfect will." The Word also tells us to think about only good things: "Finally, brothers and sisters, whatever is true, whatever is noble, whatever is right, whatever is pure, whatever is lovely, whatever is admirable—if anything is excellent or praiseworthy—think about such things" (Philippians 4:8). And we need to meditate on the Word: "but whose delight is in the law of the Lord, and who meditates on his law day and night" (Psalm 1:2).

Defeating a habit also requires changes in lifestyle. We are to make no provision for the flesh: "Rather, clothe yourselves with the Lord Jesus Christ, and do not think about how to gratify the desires of the flesh" (Romans 13:14). The person who wants to stop smoking should throw away all his cigarettes and not buy any more; the person who is struggling with sexual sin should get rid of any suggestive materials in his possession. Avoid the company of those who have the same problem: "Do not be misled: 'Bad company corrupts good character'" (1 Corinthians 15:33). Most importantly, avoid the places and circumstances that tempt you.

Finally, don't try to battle a bad habit alone. Develop relationships with mature Christians who will encourage and support you. "Carry each other's burdens, and in this way you will fulfill the law of Christ" (Galatians 6:2). Spend time in prayer with them. Give them permission to check up on you regularly, and be honest about your failures: "Therefore confess your sins to each other and pray for each other so that you may be healed. The prayer of a righteous person is powerful and effective" (James 5:16).

There's another way to eliminate bad habits and sin. Consider the pin oak, which is an interesting tree. One feature of this tree is that it retains its leaves during the winter months. I'm looking at one out our front window right now, while it is snowing, brown leaves holding tight. Though the leaves die in the fall, they remain attached to the oak's branches until the new leaves appear in the spring and push the old ones off the branch.

You could, of course, remove these leaves by hand. Think about that: pulling dead leaves off an entire tree. That would be a time-consuming and pointless exercise. The leaves will come off on their own when the new growth appears in the spring.

Bad habits are similar. You can focus your attention on eliminating them, like staring at the dead leaves still on the tree. Or, you can focus on developing positive habits. As you do so, you will naturally—and more easily—remove the bad habits. Second Corinthians 5:1 says, "For we know that if the earthly tent we live in is destroyed, we have a building from God, an eternal house in heaven, not built by human hands." In other words, like the oak leaf that comes out when replaced with a living leaf in the spring, if we "destroy" the sin and replace it with a good habit, we'll have a new building (habit) from God and that will lead toward an eternity with God in heaven.

For example, you could focus on:
- Eating tasty, fresh vegetables (adopting a good habit) instead of eliminating junk food (breaking a bad habit)
- Drinking eight glasses of water a day instead of cutting down on your coffee intake
- Complimenting your friends instead of breaking your pattern of arguing
- Reading more books instead of cutting down the time you spend surfing the Internet
- Praying for what you need instead of worrying about what you don't have
- Taking up hiking rather than changing your sedentary lifestyle

Biblical change is not just turning away from sin; it is turning toward righteousness. The person who lies must speak the truth: "Therefore each of you must put off falsehood and speak truthfully to your neighbor, for we are all members of one body" (Ephesians 4:25). One who steals must not only stop stealing, he must work and give to others: "Anyone who has been stealing must steal no longer, but must work, doing something useful with their own hands, that they may have something to share with those in need" (Ephesians 4:28). And one whose language is unwholesome must learn to edify others: "Do not let any unwholesome talk come out of your mouths, but only what is helpful for building others up according to their needs, that it may benefit those who listen" (Ephesians 4:29). Don't just stop sinning—

start doing what is right. The good habits you build will replace the sinful ones.

What good habits do you need to start building?

That moose hunting trip didn't turn out for us. The wind and rain of the week affected more than just our paddles across the lakes. It also affected the moose. They hunkered down, or couldn't hear us calling, or otherwise weren't responsive. Over the course of the ten days, Scott and I failed to see even a single moose. Dan was along tending camp and had a couple close encounters later in the week—but he didn't have a license so all he could do was enjoy seeing the moose up close.

And you know what? That's okay. We had a good time in the pursuit. We remember the days of that trip fondly. When I went along a few years later to tend camp with Dan and a couple others who were selected for a tag, I was able to see a harvested moose and share in the bounty as those guys shot a nice bull.

There may not be a next time for me in Minnesota. The season isn't open as the population in that area has declined to a dangerously low level. But that doesn't mean I might not try to hunt moose again somewhere else in the future. When I do, I'll be in my tent and I'll take the extra time to be sure I've removed as many of the sticks, stones, small roots, bumps in the ground—and even bigger rocks—that I possibly can before setting up the tent. No need to tolerate those annoyances—in camping or in life!

For Reflection ...
1. What do you consider "roughing it" when it comes to camping?

2. If you've been camping, what are your most and least favorite aspects of it?

3. What is causing some of the "bumps" in the tent you call life?

4. Have you ever been intentional about removing the sins in your life, from the smallest "pebbles" to the largest "roots"?

4
LOST LURE

I've made many trips up to Lac [Lake] Seul in northwestern Ontario, Canada. Wikipedia tells me that Lac Seul is crescent shaped, and about 150 miles long with a maximum depth of just over one hundred and fifty feet—second only to Lake Nipigon for the largest lake in Ontario. The primary focus of our trips to Lac Seul are walleye. We have our favorite places to go on the lake to catch these particular fish, but they are so abundant you could catch them just about anywhere. We've caught them in three feet of water out to forty feet during the same week. Our usual technique is a simple jig with a preserved minnow or night crawler. One of the joys of fishing on a lake with so many fish is that it gives each person an opportunity to refine his or her craft. When there are so many fish, you can get a feel for what a soft bite is like, or discern between a perch bite and a walleye bite. Even after having gone up there for many years, it is still fun for me to work at getting better at the aspects of fishing.

I was excited when my son was finally old enough to come along. I still remember Rylan's first trip to Lac Seul with me. I was not only able to work at becoming a better fisherman, but I also enjoyed watching him start to "figure it out." From tying jigs on the line, to finding the bottom with the jig, to figuring out how best to keep the bait on the hook, to discerning bite from rock—and on and on. I could see his confidence grow with the techniques, right along with my admiration as he grasped them.

When we went back the next year, he had a good sense of what the trip entailed. We both shared an anticipation of getting into the fish once again. Sure enough, we found them, and he was fishing right along beside me, Dan, and Dan's son Charlie—each holding his own while catching some great walleye. By the third or fourth day, Rylan had almost tired a bit of catching walleye. We always caught incidental northern pike while chasing walleyes, so we knew they were in there. We had also caught perch and smallmouth bass. But it was the pike that had Rylan's attention on that day. As soon as we found a spot to start chasing walleyes, Rylan grabbed a baitcaster, threw on a spinnerbait, and started throwing it toward shore.

It didn't take long for him to entice a pike to grab on. Pike are fun fighting fish when they're hooked, regardless of size, but Rylan didn't have any trouble getting this one to the boat—probably around twenty inches long, a respectable size, but nothing too big. As it was nearing the boat, someone asked if he needed the net. Because the pole he had was a bit stronger, had braided line, and he had a steel leader on his line, he could "horse" the fish in while reeling and getting it into the boat. He knew that but used the net on the fish anyway. After a moment of admiring it and getting the big spinnerbait hook out of its mouth, Rylan released it to be caught again another day.

Over the next couple hours, this repeated itself again and again. It seemed like every few casts he'd either get a hit on the lure or would actually get one to grab on and he'd have the fight on his hands. Almost immediately after he'd say he had one or someone would watch the pole bending with the weight of a fish, we'd ask "Is this one a netter?" or "Need the net?" Sometimes he would, sometimes he wouldn't. Occasionally he'd misjudge and think he had a net-worthy fish on the line, when it was actually just a little guy fighting like crazy. Whoever was netting would reel in their walleye rig and grab the net, ready to help. It was fun for everyone and always exciting to see how big his latest fish was. With walleyes, we typically had a decent idea of the fish size as soon as we set the hook. Our excitement would come when someone indicated they thought they had a nice one. With Rylan's pike, we really didn't know.

We started to get into a bit of a groove. He was catching so many that as soon as we asked if he needed a net and he'd say no, we'd generally keep on fishing and try to catch a lunker walleye of our own. After he had caught about a dozen pike, we started fishing in a new bay to see if the walleyes were in there that day. Rylan was throwing his lure again and venting a little frustration that we were out in the middle of the bay when he wanted to get closer to shore, thinking the pike would be closer to the weed edges. We were snagging some vegetation on our walleye jigs in this area, and were only in about ten feet of water, so we encouraged him to keep throwing as this was a great spot to catch a pike.

After a few casts, he had a taker and one of us asked him if he needed the net. He reeled for another second or two and said he didn't think so. It seemed to be coming in easily. Back to fishing for us. I was on the same side of the boat as Rylan and was watching as the fish was getting closer and closer to the boat. He was just reeling it right in, so I was preparing for some comment about his "little fish." The fish got within about five feet of the boat when Rylan and I saw it at the same time. And the fish saw the boat. This was no small fish. His eyes got big (mine too) and we both yelled "net!" at the same time. The three of us reeled in our lines so we could get out of the way and watch the fight. As soon as the fish saw the boat, it decided to no longer be compliant and just come on in. It was going to give Rylan a run for his money.

The fish was running under the boat, back out from where it came, and every other way it could. We helped Rylan with setting the drag on the reel so he could find that sweet spot of just enough tension so the fish couldn't spit the hook, but not too much where the line might snap. A couple times the fish made a run toward the back of the boat, so we trimmed the motor up so the line wouldn't get cut on the propeller.

I grabbed the camera to try to capture the fight. I have pictures of Rylan with the rod tucked under his arm and the pole bent down as the beast went under the boat. At one point when the fish came alongside the boat, I was able to grab a picture of its head out of the water, right before it banged on the boat and went back down. Although that picture isn't very clear, you can appreciate the size of the fish's head.

After about five minutes of fighting, the fish had enough and Charlie netted it. That proved challenging itself, though, as the fish didn't fit quite as easily into the net as our many walleye did.

For our walleye fishing, we'd typically just drop the jig over the side of the boat, find the bottom, then lift and drop the jig a few inches along the bottom until a hungry walleye would take it. It's a passive way to fish, requiring more finesse than action, but it works for that species. Rylan wanted a technique that was a little more active. He wanted to cast the lure out there and retrieve it back. Cast, retrieve. Cast, retrieve. Cast, retrieve. He kept throwing it out expecting to be hit on the retrieve. It's a busier way to fish, and considering he was catching fish regularly, it was just what he was looking for to pass the morning.

As I recall that story, I'm reminded of a verse in 1 Peter that says,

> Humble yourselves, therefore, under God's mighty hand, that he may lift you up in due time. Cast all your anxiety on him because he cares for you.
> (1 Peter 5:6–7)

In that verse, Peter is providing a clear direction to turn our anxieties—worries, cares, concerns—over to God. It doesn't say to give God only the biggest problems we have. It doesn't say to ask God to give you a hand in dealing with your worries. It doesn't say to try to fix things yourself, and if you can't, then to give them to God. Nope! It says to cast them on God.

Why would we do that? Quite simply, for the sake of freedom. We don't need to carry around those things with us. Matthew recorded Jesus telling His followers:

Come to me, all you who are weary and burdened, and I will give you rest. Take my yoke upon you and learn from me, for I am gentle and humble in heart, and you will find rest for your souls. For my yoke is easy and my burden is light.
(Matthew 11:28–30)

Jesus frees us from our burdens, whatever they may be. Jesus offers rest through love, healing, and peace with God. This doesn't mean that we don't still need to work or that we won't face challenges. But it does mean that putting your hope in Jesus—casting your burdens on Him—will provide you freedom from the things weighing you down, namely your spiritual burdens. We all have those weights around us. Regret from things you did, or didn't do, in the past. Ongoing sin or sinful desires/urges. Stress from relationships. Worries about friends or finances or health. The list goes on and on.

In his book *Crazy Love*, Francis Chan notes that:

> Worry implies that we don't quite trust that God is big enough, powerful enough, or loving enough to take care of what's happening in our lives. Stress says that the things we are involved in are important enough to merit our impatience, our lack of grace toward others, or our tight grip of control. Basically, these two behaviors communicate that it's okay to sin and not trust God because the stuff in my life is somehow exceptional. Both worry and stress reek of arrogance. They declare our tendency to forget

that we've been forgiven, that our lives here are brief, that we are headed to a place where we won't be lonely, afraid, or hurt ever again, and that in context of God's strength, our problems are small, indeed.

That's convicting. As a Christian, I think that I turn things over to God and put my trust in Him to take care of them. Or do I? Maybe I'm more like Rylan's fishing. I cast my anxieties on Him easy enough, but then I reel them back in to see if anything has changed with them. I may cast them over and over and over, each time reeling them back in to check on God's progress. It's like fishing with a bobber and a night crawler. That worm is my worry and I'm happy to stick it on a hook and cast it out. God can have it. But I'm watching the bobber the whole time for movement. And soon as it moves a little, I reel back in to see if the night crawler is still there. I cast my worry out, but then I reel it back in to see if God has taken my worry away. Is that trusting God? Is that casting my anxieties on Him? Sure doesn't seem like it.

When I was first starting to fish with a bait caster, I would tie on my lures and cast them out. More often than not, I'd end up with a fun little bird's nest of line in the reel because of my rookie use of the reel. I usually spent more time clearing the spool from line tangles than I did fishing. Every now and then, after a number of backlashes, the line would weaken in a spot or the knot I tied with my limited experience would have too much tension as the lure flew out, and the line stopped abruptly in another tangle—then the lure would go flying out into the lake without any line attached to it. Unless I was using a floating lure, the lure would sink before we could get to it and likely drift to the bottom. (The first few times this happened, I was using Dan's fishing gear and donating his lures to the lake. His patience with me can't be overstated.) We'd just chalk it up as another lost lure, re-tie, and go back to fishing. We wouldn't spend time fretting about it, but just move on. Although my plan when I was fishing was to cast and retrieve (like Rylan was doing when he caught his pike), I think God is looking for us to act more like we do when we'd lose those lures. Cast them out there like the line is broken. Forget about it and move on. No need to dwell on it. Let it be gone. Let God do His thing and take control of it. When it comes to worries, stop reeling them back in. Lose the lure.

I have pictures of Rylan and Charlie both taking turns holding the net with the big fish in it, and their expressions are priceless. As I kept snapping pictures, Dan helped get the fish out of the net, free the hook, and get Rylan ready to hold it for the "trophy" shot. Dan weighed and measured the length, then we got it back into the water—where after a few seconds, it returned to rule its domain.

The fish was right at thirty-eight inches long and weighed just under thirteen pounds. At the time, it was the biggest fish of any kind we'd had in the boat—ever. A dandy catch. Needless to say, Rylan still loves cast and retrieve fishing, waiting for the bigger fish we know are out there. Hopefully, though, he and the rest of us leave our retrieves to the fishing and learn to cast our concerns on God—without reeling them back in!

For Reflection …

1. What's been your experience with fishing? If you've been out fishing, describe your best encounter with a rod and reel.

2. Do you have a regular time each day when you talk to God? During those times, do you intentionally spend time telling Him about your worries and concerns?

3. What care have you given to the Lord that you keep wanting to reel in?

4. How patient are you with God? What do you think He wants us to learn during times that He doesn't respond when or how we think He should?

5
DON'T MOVE!

Winters in Minnesota get long—really, really long. By the time late January rolls around, and we've already had snow on the ground for a few months, and the temp is no longer climbing above zero (for the high), most Minnesotans begin dreaming of spring thaw. Spring in Minnesota can be beautiful—or maybe it's just because it isn't winter anymore that makes it seem beautiful. When the temps crawl into the thirties for the first time after the coldest temps in January and February, you'll actually find many folks out in shorts and t-shirts, desperate for the warmth.

Spring usually brings with it the messy thaw, and typically there's flooding along the major rivers as the snow melts and spring rains come. But we usually don't mind.

Those cold winters do allow us to get out on the lakes where we have so much fun in the summer chasing around crappies, walleyes, bluegills, and pike. The difference is that during the winter, we're walking on the frozen water and drilling holes to get to the fish. The ice in the northern parts of the state can reach over four feet thick. To be safe, for walking, you need about four inches of ice; driving a snowmobile or four-wheeler, eight inches; and driving a full size truck, twelve inches is a minimum.

Depending on how cold it is, we fish either on the

open ice or in fish houses. Even on extremely cold days, a small propane heater can heat up a portable fish house to t-shirt temps. Don't get me started on how folks can spruce up their permanent fish houses (those that stay in a single spot all winter long). For those, you can get satellite TV, stoves, bedrooms, stereo systems, and more.

All in all, ice fishing is good for a sportsman like me because it helps me get my fix of outdoors activity doing one of my favorite things—fishing. But when the weather starts to warm up, I don't get excited about the grass greening, or the flowers blooming, or even the water opening for boat fishing. No, for me, the spring thaw means that turkey season is coming.

Of all of the critters I hunt, the wild turkey is the only one that I can chase in the spring. I haven't taken up spring snow goose hunting, although I would like to sometime. So that leaves me with the turkeys.

In my opinion, hunting wild turkey is a combination of duck hunting and deer hunting. Like duck hunting, it helps if you're in a spot where you know the birds want to be. Like duck hunting, you put out decoys, hide in a blind, and use a call to attract the birds. But like deer hunting, you're waiting for the turkeys to walk into your decoys rather than fly. And like deer, turkeys can be wary.

One of the most powerful weapons in the turkey's arsenal of wariness is his eyesight. Like many birds, wild turkeys have phenomenal eyesight and can clearly see colors. What that means is that in order to maximize your chances of being able to harvest a turkey, you need to be dressed in camouflage clothing from head to toe, especially if you don't normally hunt in an enclosed blind.

My preferred method of hunting turkey is to go to an open area where turkeys have been using, set out a jake (juvenile male) decoy along with a hen or two, and find a tree about thirty yards away that is large enough to lean against and hide. I typically put some netting up around me so that it's just above my knee when my leg is bent, sitting on the ground. I have several cushions to sit on and lean against and settle in well before daylight and begin listening for turkeys gobbling.

I have several turkey calls. I start soft softly and progress up louder until I think the gobbling toms (adult males) hear me and are gobbling in response. In a perfect scenario, the toms will fly down to see my hen decoys and get excited, or see the jake decoy and get mad. Either way, they come running in to range of my waiting shotgun. The first turkey I shot, a nice mature tom (with spurs almost an inch long and a beard over ten inches) happened just like that. Didn't need much calling or hiding. I was sitting by an old corner post set about two yards off the field's edge, with decoys about twenty yards out. He flew down, saw my decoys, gobbled a few times, and came running. I let him strut for a few seconds, but as soon as he stopped and his head came up, he was mine.

A couple years later I took my son out to the same area. I had learned during the year after I shot the big turkey that I'd better buy some camo netting to stake in the ground around me—and that I better learn how to use a diaphragm call (mouth call). I was caught that year having to constantly put down my slate call when the turkeys were coming in to get my gun up, then reverse the process when they were going away. That's a risky thing to do given the eyesight of turkeys. I would've rather just had my gun up the whole time and been ready to shoot when they got close enough.

Anyway, Rylan and I had set up against a big tree tucked about five yards in from a forested corner that had the two outer treed edges in a bean field. I set up the decoys and staked in the camo netting around where we'd be sitting. We donned our facemasks as I started softly calling right about thirty minutes before sunrise (which is legal shooting time). The calling wasn't important in terms of getting the toms to gobble. Every dog bark in the distance or goose honk from a nearby pond got them gobbling. Then they were gobbling at each other. We felt good about the spot we were in. I was calling to help influence them toward where they should fly, when they came down from the roost. (Turkeys roost in trees at night.)

At some point near sunrise or maybe a little after, the gobbling slowed down, then crept to a stop. During that time, my calling intensified, but it was largely for my own benefit, or so it seemed, given the responses I was getting. But that didn't deter me from trying. Rylan was young then, and his patience was waning. I had a blanket along and had him sit between my legs and covered him up to help take the mid-April chill off.

It was about then that a tom gobbled. He wasn't far away. I had Rylan stay where he was while I called a bit more to see if we could pinpoint him. He gobbled again. I now knew where he was—down the field edge on the right. There was a slight hill going that way and I had positioned the decoys far enough out in the field so that they were clearly visible to a bird approaching from that way.

I stared intently in the direction from where he'd be coming, looking for any gap in the vegetation for a glimpse out into the field. Then I saw him. I can't remember if he was strutting or not, but I picked up his blue and red head and saw him gobble again. At that point I had Rylan crawl out from between my legs and onto the ground. I lifted my gun up and pointed it toward the first real opening out in front of us where I was sure he'd be coming through. I was certain he'd be focused on the decoys and just walk on by, distracted enough that I'd have a nice twenty-five-yard shot at him.

As I saw the dark shape walk down the edge of the woods getting closer and closer, I switched off my safety. He was passing behind one last overgrown clump of old fencing and barbed wire. I whispered to Rylan, who was now lying facedown at my feet, "Don't move!" This was the moment of truth. Were we camouflaged enough or would we be busted? Would Rylan stay still enough so we wouldn't be seen by those wary eyes? Was my facemask low enough over my eyes so he wouldn't spot my winter-whitened face? All questions trying to determine how well we blended in with the natural environment.

Each one of us is unique. When we're young, some folks may acknowledge that we look just like one of our parents. Later in life, it may get pointed out how much we act like one of our parents or older siblings. Usually around the teenage years is when most kids begin to lose some of their uniqueness. With the wide array of social media out there, it is just too easy for young people to see what others are doing and then, intentionally or not, try to emulate their friends. I'm not blaming social media for this, but I think it perpetuates (and amplifies) something that goes on normally. That's about the right age when kids just want to fit in. They want to be liked—and the way to do it is to follow the masses.

Unfortunately, the masses may be pursuing a path different from the one Christ has called these young people to follow. If we're honest, we know that the path of the masses is easier for kids to follow on a day-to-day basis. When these kids just want to fit in and "be popular," what motivation do they have to be different? Hold that thought.

Fast-forward a few years, or a few decades, and you will find a population of professionals who may be looking less to fit in and more to get ahead. But the way they do that isn't to stand and be different, but to separate themselves from the pack by just following a different pack. They aren't different, they're just like the ones before them who may have stepped on others to climb the ladder of success. They're pursuing the American dream of a bigger house, nicer car, more stuff—just more, more, more, more. But that's not different. That's not standing out. At least not the way the Bible tells us to.

Look at Jesus. Did He stand out? You bet He did, but not in a way that appeals to the world. Not with an active Twitter feed, or the coolest pictures on Facebook, or any other social media. He wasn't just different because He could turn water into wine, or make the leper's sores go away, or even bring the dead to life. He hung out with the wrong crowd—the troublemakers, the poor, the destitute, the foreigners, and the losers. But He wasn't hanging with that crowd or doing the miracles because He was trying to stand out. If He was trying to stand out, he would've sought company with the upper-class folks. They would have enjoyed having such powerful miracles at their disposal. Or He could have just brought the legions of angel armies to bear against the misguided rulers of the day. After all, He was God and had the authority to do that.

And then what about Stephen? This guy was being accused of things for which, if guilty, he knew the sentence was death. And what did he do? He stood his ground and preached the gospel to the Sanhedrin. In the end, he was stoned to death—but he took off his camouflage and was visible to the people around him.

How about someone who didn't do so well? Peter (after Jesus was arrested) comes to mind. Jesus had told Peter that the disciple would deny him three times before the rooster crowed. Peter adamantly resisted the idea. However, right after the arrest, Peter put on his best camouflage and tried to blend in. Questioned three times about whether or not he was with Jesus, or was one of Jesus' followers, he denied it each time. Then the rooster crowed and he realized that just as Jesus said, he was blending in—he had denied knowing Jesus.

I wonder how visible we are as Christians in our "habitat?" Do we blend in with our surroundings, trying to go undetected? When the time comes to answer to God, I would like to avoid having to answer for the times when I put on my spiritual camouflage and disappeared into the crowd—when I knew God was calling me to stand out and stand up for Him.

The Bible tells in Matthew about letting your light shine. In Matthew 5:14–17 Jesus said,

> You are the light of the world. A town built on a hill cannot be hidden. Neither do people light a lamp and put it under a bowl. Instead they put it on its stand, and it gives light to everyone in the house. In the same way, let your light shine before others, that they may see your good deeds and glorify your Father in heaven.

Isn't this the way we're called to live? Not with our light tucked under a basket—but like a brightly illuminated city on a hill that cannot be hidden. Instead of wearing our spiritual camouflage and hiding who we are in Christ, we should be letting our light shine so that all see. When they see it and ask about it, we should be ready to point them to God (This would be the part where you're "glorifying your Father in heaven.").

We need to stop being ashamed of our faith, of what gives us hope, of what guides our lives, and Who we rely on for our daily bread. We have to stop hiding among the crowd and blending in.

Note that I'm not saying we all have to grab a bullhorn and go stand on the corner of an intersection in some major metropolitan area. I've seen folks do that in downtown Minneapolis, where I work, and I'm not sure that they're being all that effective. If you feel called to do that, go to it, but that's not what I'm talking about when I challenge us to stop blending in. We don't have to go to that other extreme. Instead, let's just do what God wants us to do and not hide from it.

Our family has gone on a number of mission trips, both in the U.S. and internationally. We've asked for prayers and donations to help us prepare for each of those trips. We haven't limited the requests to just family, but have reached out to friends as well. We haven't done that for pity's sake or because we're worried about having the financial part covered. We were sure God would provide. But we've spread the word about these trips because we are not ashamed. Telling folks about what we're doing is liberating. There's a certain freedom that comes with obeying God and not shying away from telling people. We're not trying to hide that side of who we are and blend in with our "non-churched" friends. We're trying to show God's light and stand firm and unashamed in our faith. Time to shake off the camouflage and let your light shine.

As that turkey stepped into the opening, his startled head popped up and we were busted. I'm not sure what he saw, but there was no doubt that the party was over. As he spun around to get away from whatever he saw, I fired. Realize that he was only about four yards from us. At that range, his head was about three inches wide. And at that range, the pattern of my shotgun probably wasn't opened that wide yet. When hunting turkeys, you want to constrict the pattern of your shotgun as much as possible to keep a tight pattern out to longer distances. I'm sure the X-tra Full Turkey Choke that I had in my trusty Remington 870 had my pattern tight. Between that and the small target of the turkey's head, I missed. Cleanly.

Well, even with his ears ringing, he wasn't sticking around. He took off running back up the field edge. I jumped out of the blind, ran to the field edge, and fired at him twice more. He didn't crumple up. He didn't break stride. Nary a feather fell. He took off flying.

I returned to the blind. Rylan asked me if I got it or not. As I was walking to the blind, I noticed for the first time that the camouflage netting actually had two different sides. The inside of it where we were sitting was the darker side, which would have blended perfectly with our surroundings. The outside, the side we couldn't see from inside (or when we set up in the dark over an hour ago), was much lighter, appearing even as if there was snow on it. You can bet I've been more careful since then to know which side is which when I'm setting up. This time, I stuck out more than I wanted to. My attempt to blend in failed.

As I write this, I'm on an airplane, heading to San Diego for a weekend with Staci ahead of a conference where I'm speaking. Staci has several of her textbooks out, along with her Bible, as she's studying to become a pastor. Seeing those books prompted the man next to her to ask a question and now she is engaged in conversation with him. She's not hiding her faith or trying to avoid the conversation about what she's doing—or who she is living for.

Let's leave the camouflage for the turkey hunting, and

live our lives out in the open, not ashamed of the only one who offers us salvation. Let's not be afraid to talk to others about Jesus, or worry about what people might think of us if we pursue righteousness. Maybe it's time to be more like our deer hunting friends in blaze orange, visible even at dusk in the thick woods. Let's stick out and live unashamed!

For Reflection ...

1. How do you deal with the deep freeze of winter? To what do you look most forward to in spring?

2. How do we camouflage our Christian selves in our daily lives?

3. In what ways may you have caved a bit when it comes to conformity to the world's standards? What "turkeys" in your life are you hiding from?

4. What three things could you start doing today to switch from camouflage to blaze orange?

6
OUTSIDE THE WAKE

One of the best investments we've ever made is our boat. We bought it in 2006. We had never owned a boat before, so we did plenty of research before buying one. We wanted a boat large enough to hold our family plus a couple guests. We wanted to be able to fish out of it, but also pull the kids on a tube or me on skis. To be honest, I hadn't settled into fishing open water in Minnesota yet. I didn't understand how varied it could be or how to properly deck out a boat to maximize the ability to meet opportunities on big water and small. I was still a largemouth bass fisherman at heart and just knew I needed a trolling motor so I could navigate the shorelines.

Through my research, I narrowed my choices down to two different models that seemed like they'd do the trick. We weren't looking for a brand-new boat, so I spent some time on the Internet finding websites that had people trying to offload their vessels. After a few weeks, I found a couple of offers that I followed up on. After a few not-quite-right calls, I found one that seemed worth taking a look at. We loaded the family up and headed an hour north to take a look. Can't say I knew what I was looking for when we got there. I wanted to get a good read from the owner as to how it was used and if he had any problems with it. Turns out the guy who was selling the boat was the brother of the owner of the boat, but the seller fished professionally on the walleye tour, and was a wealth of information. He was the perfect guy for a first timer like me. He knew boats, he knew fishing, and he could talk about both at a level even I could understand. So we bought the boat.

It is a simple craft. A Crestliner Sportfish 1850. It has a 150 horsepower Evinrude pushing it, which can move the boat well. It also has a 9.9 horsepower "kicker" motor for slower, open trolling and a trolling motor for even slower moving about, when conditions permit it. It has a decent Lowrance combination GPS/depthfinder, two livewells, plenty of storage, and a walkthrough windshield. The bimini top comes in handy in inclement weather or when the sun is baking us in the middle of summer. There are four swivel chairs that are comfortable. One of the reasons we went with the Sportfish is the bow, which can convert back and forth quickly from a large casting platform to cushioned seats for bow riding in comfort.

The reason this boat has proven to be such a great investment is because it nudged us to spend time together as a family. Unlike a cabin on a single lake, we could go to different lakes depending on what we felt like doing. We could go out for a couple hours or for full days. We could skip weekends without feeling like we should be constantly using a much larger investment.

In 2006, the kids were nine and six years old and had much more flexible schedules than in their later teenage years, when jobs and other plans compete with family time. We would head out on the boat one or both days on most weekends. I had a general rule that we'd fish until lunch, then switch to swimming or tubing or whatever else. That worked well for me because I wasn't forced to worry about the kids on one side of the boat scaring fish on the other—and the kids had a general timeframe they could understand. It seemed like a fair deal, except on the hot days when the appeal of swimming kicked in about nine o'clock, and I would cave and just admit those were swimming days. On the other days, a pattern emerged where the kids began to want to "eat lunch" earlier and earlier in the day. Soon we were eating lunch at ten a.m. I'm convinced now it wasn't so much because of hunger, but a scheme to get Dad to put down his fishing pole and put out the swim ladder.

About a year after we got the boat, we were invited to go with some friends to an old resort in the central part of the state for a week of fishing, watersports, and hanging out. We jumped at it.

The group of folks we spent that week with have been getting together every summer since, and we consider them all among our best friends. We are blessed to have a group of friends like that where we can go a full year between visits and pick up like we saw them yesterday.

The resort had docks for boats so we took ours up and used it as much as we could throughout the week. Sometimes getting out to fish in the morning or evening, sometimes boat rides at dusk, sometimes dragging the kids around the lake on the tubes for hours in the middle of the day. Most years, the bulk of the gas I burned through in the boat was when we were tubing. I could get by with the trolling motor for most of the fishing. Cruising around the lake isn't a gas-intensive trip. Pulling the kids around on tubes, on the other hand, certainly was. But, pulling the extra weight on the back, with a tube loaded with three kids, then putting the hammer down upon receiving the thumbs up from them to go was a great use of resources. Every now and then, we'd throw two tubes back there and load them up so the kids could have tube wars, trying to knock each other off, while the boat captain was trying to make things as rough as possible for them.

When pulling a tube or two, I generally take the cue from the kids as to how crazy they want me to get. If they want me to keep crisscrossing my own wake with tight turns to get bumpy, that's fine with me. When the kids want the wilder ride, I want them to fly around and get moving fast around turns. I also take it upon myself to try to dump them from the tube. At the same time, the kids feel the challenge and want to stay on despite my best efforts. Sometimes I win, sometimes they do. My wins leave one or more riders off the tube and floating behind the boat, smiling and ready to go again. I've seen some wicked spills over the years, and even some minor scrapes, but the kids are always ready to roll the next day.

Other times the kids are a bit more timid, so I run in straight lines and let them stay in the middle of the wake where it is the smoothest. It's still fun for them in those cases. There are some rides when the folks that want to stay in the middle get caught in a bumpy area due to other boats on the lake. Sometimes you can see the tubers' faces freeze with fear and their knuckles whiten as they squeeze tighter to hang on. They want to be in the smooth part of the ride, but find themselves riding some bumpy waves that beat them up and make the ride uncomfortable.

I have to be honest, when my kids were younger and

wanted a smooth ride, I'd still push it a little bit and get them outside the wake or find some bumps for them. To be clear, my intent was to stretch them a bit outside their comfort zone—not to scare them so much they didn't want to go again. Sometimes less experienced tubers would fall off, not knowing how or when to hang on tight, and that was okay. It might have been a little fearful for them at first, but when they were done with the ride, I could see the increased confidence of having made it through. We all knew they would be better off next time.

There are many different approaches we can take to living life. We can prefer a comfortable life in the middle of the wake. We don't want to be challenged to do anything outside our simple and comfortable existence. Day to day, month to month, year to year, it remains on cruise control. And that can be okay. Remember the tortoise and the hare? Slow and steady can win the race. But taking the smooth ride *without growth*—be it professional, social, spiritual, relational, or physical—can lead to a life that is less than God has called us to live.

There will always be the "wild tubers" of the world. They challenge things every day. They live life outside the wake, bouncing around, bored if they have to ride in the smooth zone. They'll throw their weight one way or another to get the tube outside the wake so they can find life more exhilarating. Although this approach to life seems more exciting, constantly chasing the next adrenaline rush or new experience can cause people to miss the simple or obvious opportunities right under their nose—opportunities that are so important in fulfilling God's purpose for their life.

Although these two approaches to riding the tube of life seem different, there are important similarities between them as well. There are a few key components of tubing that are always present: boat, boat driver, tube, water, and the riders. Let's look closer at each of these items.

The boat is what pulls the tube through the water. There are all kinds of features to boats that can affect the ride—motor size, maneuverability, and acceleration being some of the more obvious. Boats capable of pulling a tube can be high-performance ski or wakeboard boats, cruising-around pontoon boats, or even smaller flat-bottom boats with small motors. But without a responsible driver, boats can be misused and dangerous—or sit still and unused.

Regardless of the boat, the boat driver is the one who sets the speed and course of the boat. The boat driver is responsible for taking into consideration the intended purpose and performance of the boat, the conditions of the water, and the folks being pulled on the tube. The boat driver can make the boat go faster or slower and look for rough water or smooth.

The tube essentially acts as a life preserver. Although each rider wears his or her own life vest, the tube is what they're clinging to during the ride. The tube is what makes the ride. There are times when the water may appear rough, but being on the tube can make it feel smooth. Without the tube, being dragged through the water would cause the riders to get mouthfuls of water and gasp for air.

The water can be smooth or it can be rough. Even smooth water can be made rough by the driver of the boat with enough turns and fishtailing. On the other hand, water that appears rough can be made smooth if the driver finds a calm bay for the rider or pulls the tube in the middle of the wake.

Finally, the riders can be all ages and sizes. It doesn't take any special skills or training to ride a tube. The riders simply have to trust that the tube will hold up under them and that the driver will act responsibly. Some riders jump on the tube at a young age, trusting the tube and driver without hesitation. Others have doubts about either the tube or the driver, and take a long time to build up the courage to hop on. Or they'll just stay in the boat, trusting the driver, but not the tube.

Let me give you five associations and ask that you go back and read the last five paragraphs with these new associations in mind. The boat is the plan for our lives. The boat driver is God. The tube is Jesus. The water is life. You are the rider.

It's interesting how many different kinds of boats there are, and the same boat can be used for so many different things. As I've mentioned before, my current boat is an 18-foot Crestliner Sportfish. The different motors that I have on it allow me to creep along with the trolling motor, to over 40 mph with the 150 horsepower motor full-out. We bought the boat to use for fishing big water, for waterskiing and tubing, and for just hanging out and swimming.

Someone else may have the same boat and use it only for fishing. Another person may have the same boat and use it for family water activities, never to wet a line from it. Those are not wrong uses of the boat, just different.

You see, we each have an idea of what the boat is for, and those ideas determine how we use it. We could each have them set up the exact same way and still use them differently. What changes between the uses isn't the boat, but the driver. The driver determines how the boat is used.

As we think about life plans, we can do the same thing. In Proverbs, Solomon noted that "In their hearts humans plan their course, but the Lord establishes their steps" (16:9); and "Many are the plans in a person's heart, but it is the Lord's purpose that prevails" (19:21). We make our plans to go wide open all the time. Or we make plans to take it easy, living without risks. But ultimately, God as our boat driver is the one who determines where we go.

As our driver, God may use the boat for things we had never even thought of—or He might find ways to get more of the boat than we had imagined. There will be times when God is using the boat for something we had planned for (like tubing). He'll pull us around, watching for the smiles on our faces. But He might choose to get us outside the wake. He might think that riding in smooth water in the center of the wake isn't what's best for us at the time. Maybe He wants us outside, in rough water. He might be testing us just to see if we'll just let go. He knows that riding the rough water makes us stronger and better prepared for the next ride through unsettling times.

The Bible makes several references to God "refining" us in a process similar to how impurities are removed from precious metals. Metals like gold and silver come from the ground with impurities. To remove these impurities, the metals are heated to liquid state and the impurities rise to the top to be removed. Thus, when God leads us into the furnace, His purpose is to cleanse us of impurities.

Isaiah 48:10 says, "See, I have refined you, though not as silver; I have tested you in the furnace of affliction." And Psalm 66:10 says, "For you, God, tested us; you refined us like silver." Proverbs 17:3 states, "The crucible for silver and the furnace for gold, but the Lord tests the heart." And finally, Zechariah 13:9 brings it all together and shows the benefits of God's refining us with these words: "I will refine them like silver and test them like gold. They will call on my name and I will answer them; I will say, 'They are my people,' and they will say, 'The Lord is our God.'"

Most Christians are able to understand the idea of having to face rough waters in life. We can even understand that it is for our long-term good. The verses above make it clear that God will not only let us go through those difficulties, but will often lead us into those times. Even with Him leading us, we're often still afraid of the rough water. We aren't the first people to face that fear.

Three of the four Gospels describe a time when the disciples were afraid in rough waters. Here it is from Luke 8:22–25:

> One day Jesus said to his disciples, "Let us go over to the other side of the lake." So they got into a boat and set out. As they sailed, he fell asleep. A squall came down on the lake, so that the boat was being swamped, and they were in great

danger. The disciples went and woke him, saying, "Master, Master, we're going to drown!"

Did you catch that? The disciples had Jesus in the boat with them, but they were still afraid. Oftentimes, we lose sight of Jesus and when we face rough waters, we may cry out as well, thinking we're going to drown. But Jesus' response to the disciples still applies to us today:

He got up and rebuked the wind and the raging waters; the storm subsided, and all was calm. "Where is your faith?" he asked his disciples.

Jesus still sleeps through storms. Jesus still calms the raging waters. Jesus still wonders about our faith.

When tubers are riding behind the boat and they get out beyond the wake and the ride gets bumpy, sometimes they let go of the tube, thinking that floating aimlessly in the water would be the better option. But understand that God is either taking us outside the wake or letting us be out there. During times like these, He wants us to hold tightly to Jesus. We're reminded in Hebrews 10:23, "Let us hold unswervingly to the hope we profess, for he who promised is faithful." That hope is Jesus and He who promised it is God. Holding on to Jesus will bring you peace in life because this is the same Jesus who still calms storms.

We all face questions during the storms of life: Do we trust the direction God is taking us in life? When the waters get rough, will we cling to Jesus to calm them?

Do you look back on your life and realize there are

some parts that you regret? Maybe you did or said something you wish you hadn't. Or maybe there was something that went undone that you felt you should've tried. Would you like to live the rest of your life without regrets? Think about Peter for a minute. The book of Matthew explains the way to do just that. Jesus and His disciples were on the Mount of Olives after the last supper:

> Then Jesus told them, "This very night you will all fall away on account of me" (26:31).
> Peter replied, "Even if all fall away on account of you, I never will."
> "Truly I tell you," Jesus answered, "this very night, before the rooster crows, you will disown me three times."
> But Peter declared, "Even if I have to die with you, I will never disown you" (26:33–35).

Of course, Jesus was right. In verses 69–74, Peter had three chances to align himself with Jesus, but denied knowing Him, all before the rooster crowed. Then in verse 75:

> Then Peter remembered the word Jesus had spoken: "Before the rooster crows, you will disown me three times." And he went outside and wept bitterly.

Peter felt terrible. He had denied knowing Jesus. Not just once, but three times. And that was over the course of just a few hours. He had just said that he would never disown Jesus, and he did it almost immediately after saying it. He felt so badly that he left the company of others and "wept bitterly." He regretted his actions. We won't even get into how Judas responded after betraying Jesus. Talk about regrets!

The common thread between Peter and Judas that led to them looking back on their life with regret was this: they both strayed from Jesus. They both were in the presence of the Savior of the world, of God Himself on earth, and intentionally turned their backs on Him. Both looked back on those moments with deep remorse and regret. The eternal difference between Peter and Judas is this: Peter repented and threw himself upon Christ's mercy—Judas thought he could atone for his own sin.

The path to a life without regret is simple—get near to Jesus and stay close to Him. Regardless of what challenges or temptations you may face, stay close to Jesus.

So do you have a life full of regrets? Do you let God have control of your life? Do you cling to Jesus during good times and hard times? Reflect on these questions. Think about the rough times you've faced and how you approached them. Think about the direction your life is going and whether or not you want God to drive the boat.

If you struggle with these issues but are tired of going through life without the true "Boat Captain," let me assure you that giving control of the boat to God is within your reach. Romans 10:9 says, "If you declare with your mouth, 'Jesus is Lord,' and believe in your heart that God raised him from the dead, you will be saved." If you're ready to hang on to Jesus during the times through rough waters, I'll ask that you pray this prayer now:

Dear Lord, I admit that I am a sinner. I have done many things that don't please you. I have lived my life for myself. I am sorry and I repent. I ask you to forgive me. I believe that you died on the cross for me, to save me. You did what I could not do for myself. I come to you now and ask you to take control of my life, I give it to you. Help me to live every day in a way that pleases you. I love you, Lord, and I thank you that I will spend all eternity with you. Amen.

There is one constant to tubing: Whenever the rider falls off, the driver always goes back to get them. Their life vests can keep them afloat for a while, but they're at the mercy of the waves and could get run over by other boats. Similarly, life riders may fall off or let go of Jesus at times when life gets too bumpy—or they want to test God to see if He'll come back to get them. Rest assured that God will always come back to get us. He'll offer the opportunity to climb into the boat or to get back on the tube. Sometimes I think He's driving around the lake just looking for people to get on the tube. Like all responsible boat drivers, God loves to see the smiles on the riders' faces when they're hanging on to the tube, secure in Him as they ride the waves.

For Reflection ...

1. What are your favorite water activities?

2. If your life was a tube ride, would it be more behind the boat or outside the wake?

3. When your life is "outside the wake" and you feel out of control, what do you cling to?

4. Why would God intentionally get you outside the wake? How can you be more comfortable out there?

7
UPHILL, BOTH WAYS

The Boundary Waters Canoe Area Wilderness (BWCA) sits on the border between northeastern Minnesota and Canada. The southern edge of the BWCA is accessible via a series of gravel roads. Depending on who you talk to, most travelers enter either from the Ely area (west side) or from the Grand Marais side (east side). Entering the BWCA isn't like driving through a gate or crossing a bridge. It's far more primitive than that. Established in 1964 under The Wilderness Act, the heavily forested and lake-covered area is over one million acres in size and offers canoe (or snowshoe) and camping opportunities for recreationalists year round.

My first trip into the BWCA was in 2003, and with the exception of one year, I've gone every year since. There's something about having to pack everything you need into waterproof bags that fit on your back that resonates with me. I appreciate the solitude and raw beauty of the area. Cooking freshly caught fish over a campfire. Seeing stars like you can see in few other places. All of that is as impressive as it sounds. But what often gets me is the way that, on any given day, you can come face to face with your physical limits. There's no motor or roof or air conditioner or cell phone that can help you. You just need to dig deep and man up.

Maybe it's that attraction that made my fourth trip

into the BWCA so memorable. We typically drive up to my friend's house in Eveleth, about an hour or so from Ely, on Thursday afternoon. Friday morning, we leave early, grab some bait in Ely, and push off, coming back out on Monday. Not a long trip, but enough to "find ourselves." My fourth trip into the BWCA was in 2006. I met my friend on the northern side of the Twin Cities and we began the three-hour trip to Eveleth. A year prior a friend and I had built a canoe rack for my truck. It was simple, but could easily hold two canoes and proved itself handy during our 2005 trip. I'd made that drive many times over the years since Dan moved his family to Eveleth, and I knew that when we left Interstate 35 at the exit for Highway 33 at Cloquet, we were less than an hour away.

All was going smoothly as we approached the intersection in Cotton, Minnesota. We're under thirty minutes until our arrival. And then ... *BANG!* The truck decelerated, although the cruise control had the engine still revving. I guided it to the side of the road, looked in my rearview mirror and saw all kinds of smoke.

I'm not that handy with mechanical things. I'm a biologist, so never needed to be. But even I know that when the vehicle is in gear and you push on the accelerator, and the vehicle acts like it is in neutral, you've got a transmission problem. I didn't have a transmission problem, actually. I no longer had a transmission. It was done. My truck had recently celebrated its 100,000-mile birthday and this is how we decided to party.

About an hour later we were met by the towing company representative from Virginia. He wondered what was wrong with it. I mentioned that the transmission was blown. "Start it and try to pull forward." "You can hear the motor revving and see the truck sitting there, can't you?" So he looked underneath and said something to the effect of "Yep, you're done!" He loaded it up on the flatbed, with us in the cab of the tow truck, and off we went to one of the dealerships in Virginia.

At the time, Dan was driving a mid-1990s model Explorer. It had a roof rack that was perfect for his canoe. However, on this trip, it was going to be three of us, and we had a normal canoe and a solo canoe. (The solo canoe is shorter and has the seat more toward the center to allow better control by a single paddler.)

We played with the idea of rigging both canoes on the luggage rack on top, but couldn't get that to work. Our Plan B was to slide the solo canoe in through the open window in the back of the Explorer and pack our stuff around it. That would work. We didn't have that far to go.

Somehow I drew short straw and ended up packed in the back seat with the solo canoe, and far more gear than necessary for three guys going in for only a few days. I wouldn't have minded that so much, except that the morning temperature was about 38 degrees. We had packed that stuff in the cargo area of the truck. The front of the canoe, where we folded down the other seat, directed the freezing wind that came in the open window right into my lap. I was cold.

When we got to Ely and stopped by the gas station/bait shop, I bought some neoprene gloves. Not so much for the weather we were facing, but to try to warm up before we got to the access point. It was also raining off and on during our drive from Eveleth to Ely. Mid-30s with a cold rain is just about the most miserable weather conditions known to man.

We arrived at our entrance point. The plan was to put in at Snowbank Lake, paddle and portage our way up to Knife Lake, and spend a couple days chasing lake trout. We completed the short portage with the canoes and gear, and loaded up. Dan set out in the solo canoe, and our other friend Tom and I in the regular canoe.

Snowbank Lake is right on the edge of the BWCA and allows 25 horsepower and smaller motors on it. To the layman, that means it's a sizeable lake. We weren't intimidated by paddling across big lakes. But, it is under 40 degrees outside, steadily raining now, with winds right around 20 mph. Winds that high on a large lake can create some intimidating waves. We knew the portage out of the lake and the continuation of our journey was on the other end of Snowbank. There's a large island in the middle of the lake and so we made our way toward it. We'd be able to move along the eastern edge of the island and gain at least a little protection from the northwest wind.

We made it safely to the island and paddled along for a while. We even took a break there. We were a little worn out already from the constant paddling. Honestly, we also needed to pull together a little bit and all rely on each other for a little boost of courage before continuing. We reminded ourselves that the lake trout should be biting when we got to Knife Lake and it would be worth the trip.

Life jackets back on over all of our rain gear, dry bags rechecked, and away we went. When we left the cover of the island, the waves were everything we thought they'd be. It was during this paddle from the cover of the island to the portage that the rain switched to sleet. Wind-blown sleet feels like little needles piercing your skin. For us, the only exposed skin was on our faces. It was getting downright painful now. Aside from the stress of the paddling against the wind, and worrying about the waves, we now were being bombarded by ice darts. Awesome!

We eventually made it across the lake and located the portage. In the years prior to this one, we had seen our share of portages. Some were short, some long. Some flat, some steeper. There were muddy ones, rocky ones, smooth ones, and downright beautiful ones. In most of the cases up until this trip, when we stepped out of the canoes at the portage landing, the portage itself was usually level. There we could unload, gather the gear, and begin the trek to the other side where we would reload the canoes and keep going. On this one, however, things were different. We found that the subsequent portages on this trip were fairly similar.

What we found on this set of portages was that they were not so much gradual landings with easy unloading spots or flat areas to grab the gear and/or canoes to begin the portages, but instead were more like elevated lakeshores. It seemed like we would see the trail from a ways out (through the sleet), but as we paddled up to it, we realized that the beginning of the trail was at eye level. We were sitting in the canoes, looking up at the trail. Somehow, we had to get one of the paddlers out of the canoe and carefully unload the canoe without tipping it. Then we had to pull the canoe up onto the bank and begin the portage. All challenging enough, but that wasn't the full extent of it. Turns out this particular set of portages were unique in another way too. Within about five steps of walking away with gear on our backs, the portages became steep—and uphill.

Have you ever heard someone mention that back when they were kids, they "had to walk to school uphill, both ways, in the snow, barefoot"? Well, it wasn't snowing and we had boots on, but these portages were definitely uphill. Considering that each portage took two trips from each of us, we had to go up and down to the other side, turn around and go up and down to gather the remaining gear, then up and down again so we could press on—it was in fact uphill both ways.

Press on? Is it worth it? This trip to the wilderness isn't much fun. It isn't very relaxing. We're not even sure we're going to catch any fish to eat. If we don't die of exhaustion, then hypothermia or starvation will get us for sure. Whose idea was this anyway? Can't we just turn back?

We didn't turn back. I don't turn back. I work out and consider myself pretty fit. I run most mornings, and have lifted weights for over twenty years. I feel like I'm strong enough and nimble enough to take on any terrain or conditions. I'm never the first to back down from a physically grueling task and feel like I'd stand firm in the face of any realistic danger a suburbanite like me might face. I have this little nagging voice in my head that feels the need to know how far I can go. So a trip like this is perfect for a guy like me.

A few of my favorite Bible verses come from the book

of Joshua. Joshua was chosen to lead the Israelites across the Jordan River and into the Promised Land. They had been wandering around the wilderness (that is, dry desert, not icy northern Minnesota lakes) for forty years. They'd been whining and complaining more than anything. God said it was finally time to have them take over the land He had promised to Moses. As God is encouraging Joshua to prepare him to cross the river, He tells him three times (Joshua 1:6, 7, 9) to "be strong and courageous." Three times over the course of four verses. You don't need an advanced degree in theology to realize that anytime something is repeated in the Bible, it's a good sign that it's important. God just said it three times in four verses. We'd better sit up in our chairs and listen when He does that.

Note that He didn't say "Go be nice and polite." Or "Go ask for the bad people to leave." Or "Be timid and weak." No, He said to "Be strong and courageous." He said it multiple times because He knew the hard part was coming. The Israelites were going to have a fight on their hands.

The command to "be strong" can be misunderstood. All of the guys who lift weights for the big muscles can take this to mean drive fast, live dangerously, and lift weights for a commanding presence. That is not what God meant when He told Joshua to "be strong." The command was aimed at strength of character and conviction.

Here's a fun little word that points to conviction: *sticktoittiveness* (stick-to-it-tiveness). It means, to finish the task, to drive through discomfort to achieve a goal, to face hard times or troubles and keep going. Proverbs 24:10 says, "If you falter in a time of trouble, how small is your strength!"

If faced with a difficulty, do you turn back with small strength or do you face it head on, break out the "big strength" and push through?

What about courage? Does that mean I have to run into burning buildings, or jump out of airplanes, or track down international terrorists? Some of those things scare me. How can I be courageous if I'm afraid? I like this definition: *Courage isn't the lack of fear; it's doing what needs to be done despite the fear you feel.* I can relate to that. I can overcome fear for a greater good.

How strong and courageous is enough? How high is the bar set? In today's world, will I really ever be challenged in that strength or courage? Can't I just avoid trouble and play it safe? Probably, but then I'll never know what I'm capable of doing, or what the limits of my courage and strength might be.

Too many folks sit back and take it easy. Turn on the air conditioning, recline on the couch, and watch the big screen. I enjoy that too, sometimes. The problem is, when that's *all* that people do, how do they know what they're truly capable of? How do they know their point of exhaustion? How do they know if that burning in their legs or lungs or arms is nothing to worry about—or if they are at a point where they're about to pass out? Don't you want to know what you can handle, how far you can go, how long you are able to withstand the rigors of life?

You see, in facing these physical and emotional challenges, I'm not just figuring out my limits, I'm developing character. I'm developing a sense of trust in my abilities. I have a new faith in my body. When I know those things, I'm then ready to take on more. To press harder. To get to that limit of endurance and push it a little longer. The next time, when things are harder or heavier or longer or steeper—I'll be ready.

In 2 Corinthians 11, the apostle Paul explains a series of hardships he's gone through. They make my wilderness challenges seem petty. He writes to the church in Corinth:

> I have worked much harder, been in prison more frequently, been flogged more severely, and been exposed to death again and again. Five times I received from the Jews the forty lashes minus one. Three times I was beaten with rods, once I was pelted with stones, three times I was shipwrecked, I spent a night and a day in the open sea, I have been constantly on the move. I have been in danger from rivers, in danger from bandits, in danger from my fellow Jews, in danger from Gentiles; in danger in the city, in danger in the country, in danger at sea; and in danger from false believers. I have labored and toiled and have often gone without sleep; I have known hunger and thirst and have often gone without food; I have been cold and naked (2 Corinthians 11:23–27).

Those are real challenges. Those build character. The thing is, he wasn't doing those things to find out how much he could handle. He wasn't trying to be ready for the next challenge. Paul was sacrificing his life for the gospel—to spread the news of Jesus as far as he could to reach as many people as he could. As the *Life Application*

Study Bible points out in reference to Paul's list of hardships, "the trials and hurts we experience for Christ's sake build our character, demonstrate our faith, and prepare us for further service to the Lord."

Paul was being used to his maximum, by God. The more he was persecuted and suffered, the more God used him. The more he built his character and demonstrated his faith by enduring those trials and tribulations, the more God knew he could take—and the more He used him to reach people with the gospel. For Christians just starting out, that can be intimidating. I get the idea of sharing my hope with others and the call to spread the gospel, but do I have to be shipwrecked and starving to do it? Of course not. But go do something. Start small, but go.

Get involved in serving at your church, at the local homeless shelter, at the food pantry, or at the nursing home in your town. Start serving others and, as you do, God will put opportunities in front of you to share the gospel.

At first you'll think that you won't know what to say, or that you don't know your Bible well enough to talk to people about Jesus. Start small. Help an elderly lady with her groceries and say "God bless" as you walk away. Buy a homeless person a meal and say "God told me to get your dinner." You'll bite your tongue and keep your eyes straight ahead next time you're cut off, and tell your friend in the passenger seat that "God wants us to forgive others."

These small acts will cascade into bigger actions as you show God you're ready. You need to build your Christian character and demonstrate faith—and you do that by being strong and courageous. Trust that God will have your back.

As we cleared those portages and paddled, we finally reached Knife Lake, our final destination. The first three campsites we passed were occupied. To be honest, we were beat. A good fire, warm meal, and toasty sleeping bag sounded good. It wasn't raining too hard when we finally found an open campsite. We set up our tents, hung a tarp over the fire pit, and gathered the driest wood we could find.

Just because the campsites are considered primitive in the BWCA, doesn't mean we can't use lighters to try to start a fire. Believe me, we tried. Seemed like every piece of wood we touched was soaked through and did not want to burn. We had rigged a makeshift clothesline under the tarp but above the fire pit in hopes of drying out our clothes a bit from the warmth of the fire. We ended up hanging our wet socks over the flame of the packable camp stove, while we cooked sausages to just above freezing so we could get some food in our systems. Tom crawled into his sleeping bag and we didn't see him again for sixteen hours.

The next morning came a bit brighter. It was still overcast, but the rain stopped. We were able to get a fire going (more from clearer heads than drier wood) and our spirits instantly rose. We had all of our rain gear hanging over the fire, as well as more wood stacked on top of the cooking grate to help dry it out.

Dan and I set out to an island, tried unsuccessfully for some lake trout, had a fun encounter with a moose, and headed back to camp, catching a smallmouth bass on the way so we could eat.

The next day we paddled part of the way out and stopped on Ensign Lake. We saw the sun that day and caught quite a few walleyes for dinner. Mosquitos put us to bed early. Although we had all regained feeling in our feet by then, we were still ready for a nice night of rest.

The trip finished out fine from there. We stopped by the dealership in Virginia on the way home and picked up my truck and its new ($2,000) transmission.

The next time I face a battle like that, or one with even higher winds and waves, sharper sleet in my face, and steeper portages, I'll be ready! I've progressed through the small steps of faith that I've taken. The next time I'm facing a battle to do more for the kingdom, I'll know that God has developed a strong and courageous character in me, and I'll step up to the challenge.

For Reflection ...

1. Where do you draw the line when it comes to your physical limits? What's a small thing you could do to stretch that line out a bit?

2. Have you ever been tempted to give up? If so, what happened?

3. Are you living your life so full of "stuff" that every day feels like you're testing your limits? If so, what can you do right now to make a change?

4. If you pushed your limits in a healthy way, what do you think God could use you for? What do you think God wants you to be ready for?

8
TRIPLE TRIPLE

Without a doubt, bird hunting remains at the top of my list of favorite outdoor activities. Yes, hooking into a meaty walleye or having a largemouth bass hit a crankbait is fun. The excitement of seeing and shooting a deer with a bow will rattle the nerves of even the most experienced hunter. Sitting around a fire in the middle of the Boundary Waters Canoe Area Wilderness after a successful day of fishing is fantastic.

But there's something special about bird hunting. Maybe it's because you don't have to worry about scent control like you do with deer. Maybe it's because you're not confined to a small platform, or at the mercy of a boat motor, or a finicky fish to find your offering appealing. Those are valid reasons. I think it's more about enjoying the company of others, watching good dogs at work, and, most of all, the anticipation that every next step could have the grassland erupting with a pheasant—or the next second could have a flock of ducks buzzing the decoys from the one area you weren't watching. And, of course, the fact that you always have to be ready!

It was during one of our annual trips to North Dakota chasing waterfowl and upland birds that I noticed I had a crack in my truck's windshield that was quickly expanding across the window. Parking outside at the motel in the freezing weather, then bouncing around on the rough roads didn't help either. We had a few days left and I was getting nervous about how fast the crack was expanding, so I made the decision to get the windshield fixed. I was able to track down a windshield repair company out of Jamestown who was willing to meet me halfway between their place and Ellendale (where we were staying). Right after our morning pheasant walk, Dan and I, with dogs in the back, set off for the meeting place. We met the gentleman at the agreed upon gas station and ate a bite inside during the hour or so it took him to replace the windshield. He finished it up, I paid him, and we started the hour or so drive back.

It's important to understand that when we'd hunt in North Dakota, we'd rarely take paved roads. You see, unless the land is posted with no trespassing signs, the land is open for hunting. If we spotted a rooster pheasant run across the road into a parcel of land that wasn't posted, we'd jump out where we saw it, and walk into the ditch to see if we could get the bird up. (Note: We made sure it was safe in that there weren't any cars coming, and there weren't homes or livestock nearby.) I'd say we were successful about a quarter of the time. Either the pheasant would jump before we were out of the vehicle, or it would fly toward the truck or in some unsafe shooting direction, or the bird would just disappear as only a pheasant can do.

We have logged a bunch of miles around Ellendale and knew the spots where birds commonly could be found along the roads. We were familiar with all the unposted land spots too. But we were coming down from an area where we hadn't been before, on unfamiliar roads. It had been a dry summer and fall, so we didn't have to worry about mud. But there were places where it seemed like there would be roads, and then they magically evaporate into a field, or stop at a house, or run straight into a huge wetland. We had done well on this drive, adding a couple roosters to our bag. There was one I winged that my yellow lab had to chase several hundred yards down a cut corn field before catching it. That's a magical story in itself.

As we pressed on along one of those "is this a road or not?" thoroughfares, we bumped into a small flock of Hungarian partridges (or huns). These birds are about the size of a pigeon, but they fly like a quail. They hang out in small groups and can explode from their hiding spot and get out of range before you can blink. This group of about eight birds did what most flocks of huns do, namely, fly a little ways as a group, and then land. Fortunately for us, the way this group flew was up the road, and where it landed, was near a spot with bare ground and only a small clump of vegetation. Easy for us to know where they were and plan our attack. That didn't mean we had much time, though.

Dan's semi-auto shotgun hadn't been cycling through its shells recently, so he grabbed my backup (a pump), I grabbed mine, and away we went. We were walking at a good speed and developing our plan as we went. We were walking on the side of the road opposite the birds. When we arrived across from the clump where we thought they were, we crossed the road. As we came across the road,

Dan was on my right, and as expected, the clump erupted with birds.

I was tracking about five of them that got up flying away from us. I quickly got on one of them and fired. As I shot and the bird fell, two of the remaining birds turned left. I pumped my shotgun and, as the bead of my gun passed through the trailing bird, I fired again. That bird crumpled too. I pumped my last shell into the chamber without even lowering my gun, caught up with the last bird and pulled the trigger. That bird, like the last two, crumpled on the shot.

I'd been bird hunting long enough to know that when you're in a group and birds get up, it's usually a free-for-all with legal birds being fair game for all shooters. I had assumed that Dan had been shooting along with me and perhaps had shot at the same birds I did, so I wasn't sure I had just scored an elusive triple on huns. I turned to ask Dan what he hit. Dan was standing there, trying to get a shell in the chamber or get the safety off—I wasn't really sure. The one thing I do know is that he didn't shoot. In a matter of just a few seconds, I had tracked a group of flushing birds, focused on three individuals in the group, swung cleanly through three of them, and successfully knocked each of them down with each of my three shots.

We gathered the birds, got back in the truck, and again set off for Ellendale. Along with the retrieve my lab had made a little while earlier, I was feeling like an efficient hunter for the rest of that day and slept with a big smile on my face that night. After all, that was my first clean triple—fast, efficient, and effective. There wasn't time to think. Just act. Or better said, *react*.

When we hunted pheasants on our trips to North Dakota, we used every trick we knew. We'd do the standard line-up in a large field and walk across, spaced by about twenty yards, with the dogs out in front. We'd try "swinging gate" types of formations to push the birds to the edges. We'd walk the edge of cattails while some guys staggered ahead for the wild flushing roosters (You have to be careful with this formation as your hunting partners are in front of you.). As I mentioned earlier, we'd drive the roads looking for the careless birds running across the road.

There was one particular set of tree lines where one intersected another longer tree line, forming a "T" with a longer crossarm. To hunt this area, a couple guys would start off at the bottom of the "T" and walk up it toward the intersection, pushing birds in front. Another group would start at one end of the crossarm and would also walk toward the intersection. Finally, a group would wait at the other end of the crossarm as blockers. The theory was that some birds would run in front of the two groups of pushers and erupt out the end with the blockers. We'd had some success with this method in the past. It was a windy day and we thought the birds might be hunkering down in the tree lines. There were six of us in our group and we had five roosters in the bag already.

Dan and I didn't like to block, but we agreed to this time. It involves a lot of standing around for a while on a hunt like this one and we wanted to be moving. As the two groups of pushers started walking, we were milling around a bit at our blocking spots and decided to walk a fence line across the road from tree line. I had one of my labs out and she got birdy almost as soon as we started along the fence line. I was expecting a bird to get up almost immediately, as excited as she was. As she picked up the pace along the fence, I did too. Dan was coming behind me and we were ready for a bird to bust out of cover.

As we crested a small hill, there was a spot where water had gathered in the spring. I figured the bird the dog was chasing was going to be hiding in there. She hit the edge of the weedy patch and it erupted. There were pheasants everywhere. And best I could tell, most of them were roosters.

As with the huns, I quickly found one getting up and with a shot of the reliable pump, he piled up. I switched to the next long-tail I saw, pushed my bead through his flight and shot again. He fell too. I cycled the pump one more time, found a third ringneck fleeing the scene, tracked him, got in front of him a little, and pulled the trigger. Bird down! Did that just happen?

I again asked Dan about what he shot. He didn't pull the trigger. When my lab took off down the fence, he lagged behind just enough that he wasn't able to get a shot at any of them. I had just tripled again. This time on long-tails. My lab made quick work of the three retrieves, although the second one had burrowed in a little, but not far enough. She found him and I had my three roosters, the daily limit.

We quickly returned to our blocking posts, and by the time the pushers got to us, the rest of the group had their remaining birds and our collective eighteen-bird limit for the day.

Having the dog along certainly helped me know that a bird was in the cover somewhere, but the dog couldn't tell me that she smelled more than one, or that this small weedy patch was about to erupt with over a dozen roosters. Those three shots took less than five seconds. In that case, like with the huns, I just had to react.

I've had the great fortune of hunting with a group of guys in North Dakota who I consider among my best friends. We get along well and almost every decision is made by committee. With no obvious "leader" we all can contribute to designing hunting plans and find that we end up successful most of the time because the discussion allows us to maximize our collective knowledge of hunting.

There is one thing that Dan and I find ourselves deferring to our friends for regularly, though. That is, where to set up for ducks. Our friends are avid waterfowlers. The late afternoons we spend looking for careless roosters running across the road, these guys spend with their eyes in the sky looking for "the spot." That spot consists of a field where flock after flock after flock of ducks pours in. There may also be geese in the area, but those aren't usually the target of their quest. Our friends just have the knack for finding the specific field the birds are dumping into.

Where we hunt, the ducks will head out from their loafing water later in the afternoon and go to a field to feed. They'll stay in the field until around dark or a little later, then return to the water to spend the night. The next morning, they head back out to feed, usually starting where they ended the night before. They also have an uncanny ability to return to the exact spot where they left. If you can be in that spot with some cleverly placed decoys, they'll dump in, assuming they're late to the party and trying to catch up on feeding. We've ambushed many an unsuspecting flock of ducks this way.

Our friends know this well and will spend a great deal of time viewing a field being used by ducks to determine the exact knoll or low spot in a field where the ducks are landing in the late afternoon. When these guys say they've found the spot, we don't argue. Too many times, they've put us in fields with ducks literally trying to land on our feet. So we just lay still in our mummy-like layout blinds until this happens.

The other thing these guys have is a trailer full of decoys. Full-size decoys. Extra-large decoys. Spinning-wing decoys. Decoys that spin or sway in the wind. Ducks. Geese. You name it, these guys have it. And a lot of them. I'm blessed to have friends with this much gear.

We returned to the house we were renting one evening to have dinner together. The guys told us of a field they found. It sounded like a classic. Birds dumping in. Messy cut corn, but not down to just stubble, so we could hide. They had a good handle on where to set up. And although not required, since the field wasn't posted, they had secured permission to hunt in the field.

The next morning found us setting up in the location they had marked in their mind. All of the decoys were set out. The blinds were well camouflaged and it was still dark. Perfect!

As the eastern sky began to glow, we settled into our blinds and watched the show. Birds began to leave the water they were roosting on and began filtering in. Some small groups, some larger. We generally like to shoot just drakes (males) and, until the sun gets up a little higher, telling the difference when looking at backlit birds can be tough. We had shot a couple birds that different guys were sure were drakes, but hadn't all shot at a group yet. It just wasn't quite bright enough to pick out the drakes.

Every now and then, there would be a different duck call than the mallard quacks we were getting used to. Either a pintail or a widgeon would be coming through. If we could pick them out, we'd go ahead and shoot. Again, not very easy with the little light we had.

Then a larger group of widgeon came through. Their whistle call is distinct and their smaller size is easy to pick out when compared to mallards. We had several groups circling by now, but we kept track of the widgeon. We were all getting antsy to shoot as a crew and knew the widgeon was our chance. They made one pass. Then another. After that second pass, we agreed that if they came back through and were going to sit, we'd shoot.

On that next pass, they still didn't come in the way we like, centered on the decoys and our layout blinds, which would have given everyone a good opportunity to shoot. Instead, they came across the decoys and sat on the left side of the spread. That happened to be my side of the spread. As they were sitting down, I said "I'm shooting" and sat up in my blind. (In order to be transparent here, I shouldn't have sat up or shot. I was hunting in a group and when just one gunner "goes hot" in a group, that tends to rob others of the opportunity. To this day, I kick myself for that decision.)

As I sat up in my blind, the birds kept flying. This particular group was coming in, that is, landing, so they were dropping in elevation and coming across (moving right to left). Picture a smaller target, coming in fast, moving over and down in an unpredictable manner. When they get ready to land, they tend to put their brakes on over the field, and may hover for a minute, or move laterally as they figure out the spot they want to land. It's still dark too. And I said "I'm shooting"? What was I thinking?

When fowl hunting, you can't always know where the bird will come from. You need to practice shooting so you get comfortable making all kinds of shots. Dropping in. Raising up. Left to right. Right to left. And any combination of those scenarios.

Then add in some complexities. For example, you never know beforehand what the bird's flight will look like. When shooting at a trap range, you have a good idea of what the clay target will do. In hunting, that's not often the case, unless you hunt with pointing dogs and can anticipate where the bird is and where it'll fly—even these scenarios aren't that easy.

Then you need to walk and be ready. Or sit up in a blind and be ready. But you still don't know how the birds will react when you walk up on them or when you sit up.

All you can do is prepare with enough practice, so you're ready for as much as possible.

The temptations we face can be like this. We go through life without knowing where they'll come from or when they'll arrive. Temptations catch us off guard, and without being prepared, we don't know how to avoid them or how to shoot them down. Consider this: You're in class taking a test and the student next to you, the smart one, is sitting in such a way that you can see his answers clearly. And he's on the page that you're struggling with the most. What are you going to do? Look at it?

Or consider this: You're a person who likes to drive seven miles an hour over the speed limit. Today you've increased it by a little and you didn't see the policeman until he had his lights on behind you. He walks up to the car and asks a simple question: "Do you know how fast you were going?" In that moment, you know you set the cruise control for ten over the limit. But do you answer the way most people do and say no, hoping your act of ignorance will buy you some leniency?

You're hunting for pheasants and see a few roosters run across the road onto private land from the public land you were checking out. You think they're right next to the road and you're out in the middle of nowhere. You can be in there and out in just a few minutes. Do you go?

You didn't expect these situations to come up. You haven't considered them or made decisions ahead of time on what you'll do. So how are you going to react? Looking at the paper, lying to the officer, and trespassing certainly break the rules of the world—but don't they also violate the standards God has called us to live by?

What about the temptation to ignore or avoid doing the right thing? You get the weekly e-mail from the church that lays out all of the remaining service spots they need filled for the weekend. You've ushered before, but this isn't your week and you want to sleep in on Sunday morning. How do you reply?

Your elderly neighbor can't mow his yard anymore. You see he's hired a yard service to come take care of it. Money is short for him, but you're glad they have their yard work covered by someone who can handle it. Shouldn't you just make the time to take care of it for free?

Same with the widow or divorced mom across the street after a snowstorm. She can shovel her driveway just fine. It is cold out and you have your whole driveway and the sidewalk to clear with your snowblower. You just want to get back inside to warm up and watch the game. Do you finish your side and call it good?

Those temptations are no different from the seductive websites that you know you shouldn't be viewing, or infidelity, or stealing money. People face temptations all the time, and what may seem like an easy temptation to overcome might be difficult for someone else. For each individual there is a gradient of how difficult certain temptations are to resist—but a temptation is a temptation.

Jesus took on Satan for forty days in the wilderness, facing temptation after temptation. You'll see that Jesus resisted temptation from Satan because He was prepared by studying and relying on the Word of God. He recited Scriptures as retorts for each of the temptations He knew that He'd eventually face. Jesus immersed Himself in the Scriptures as He was growing up. Maybe Joseph and Mary had a worn-out copy of "The Children's Book of The Law" that they read to Jesus when He was young. They would have told him stories of Adam and Eve, Noah, and Moses, perhaps with the color pictures of the garden and the apple and snake, the ark and all of the animals, and the wall of water as Moses and the Israelites fled Pharaoh through the Red Sea. As Jesus got older, they may have given Him His own "Student Study Book of The Law" that He carried through the teen years and read from when He met His buddies for devotions. As He moved into His twenties, maybe He used His own money to go buy His own copy of the adult-age-level version of "The Book of Law, including the Prophets."

Whatever He did, He was ready to face the temptations that Satan brought into the wilderness by relying on the Word of God. So how do you prepare for the temptations that are going to come your way? Practically speaking, you need to prepare the same way Jesus did. You need to get into the Bible and not just to read, but to study, pore over, reread, learn, and memorize.

You can start with finding verses that help you through temptations you know will come. Just like practicing shots at clay targets that replicate the shots you expect in the field, you can have those anchor verses memorized to rely on to help you through your anticipated temptations.

That's a great starting spot. You can prepare even more by spending time with others who are grounded in the Bible, in small groups, and reading books based on biblical principles. As you overcome those regular temptations to sin, you develop faith not only in yourself but also in God. Then, when the surprise temptations come, you'll know that, with God's help, you can beat those too. Remember 1 Corinthians 10:13: "No temptation has overtaken you except what is common to mankind. And God is faithful; he will not let you be tempted beyond what you can bear. But when you are tempted, he will also provide a way out so that you can endure it." That means He has already given you the wherewithal to withstand any of the temptations that you'll face.

Further, in 2 Thessalonians 3:3, Paul wrote, "But the Lord is faithful, and he will strengthen you and protect you from the evil one." We all like the "protect" part of that Scripture. Some folks mistakenly think that when they accept Jesus as Savior they'll have an easy life, free of those temptations. I've read through the Bible a few times and I haven't seen anything that says once you become a follower of Jesus life will become easy. No, temptations still come. As we mature in our faith, God will "protect" us by giving us the tools to resist them. However, the other part of that Scripture also resonates with me. It says God will "strengthen and protect" us from Satan. That means that God will give us power to fight with Him against the devil's attacks. We aren't to sit back and just ask God to remove whatever challenges or temptations we may be facing. Instead, we're to be active in standing strong. God will "strengthen" us to fight back.

In the temptations or sins that I've been resisting since realizing how much I need Jesus, I can look back and see how my prayers have changed as I've matured in my faith. I've gone through a progression, beginning with a request for God to remove this burden from me. It sure would be easy if God would just close my eyes to sharply dressed women. Or if He would just take my sense of pride from me and replace it with humility. But those early prayers went largely unanswered.

The next phase of my prayers went more like this: "God, I ask you to give me the power to face these challenges so I can overcome these temptations." Then I started saying prayers like "God, without you, I can't do anything, but with you we can do anything and I'm sure ready to fight the fight with you." That's the one that fits along nicely with the 2 Thessalonians passage that reminds us that God protects me *and* strengthens me to fight the evil one.

Interestingly, as I prayed about this verse one morning, I felt as if God was reminding me that He'd always be there for me and with me. In addition, He also "suggested" that I avoid the temptations in the first place. It's like the big mouth in school who keeps starting fights he can't finish and runs home to his father to protect him. The father keeps coming out to keep his son from getting pummeled, every time. And he would continue to do so. But eventually the dad tells his son that life might be a bit more peaceful if he'd stop running his mouth and picking fights. What a novel idea! Just avoid the temptations in the first place. Don't hang out with those friends who want to steal. Don't go into that bar when you know you can't avoid drinking. Don't get on the Internet when the draw of pornography is too strong. Be a wise son and stop running your mouth so "Dad" doesn't have to keep saving you.

Do good and right things *on purpose*. Once you learn to make the obvious shots for hunting standing still, then, with practice, you'll be able to make those shots while walking. By doing the good things regularly, you'll start seeing opportunities to do the right thing in places you hadn't recognized before. You'll begin embracing those too, thereby resisting the temptation to avoid doing that thing. That's the practice. You can always bring along the right weapon and the right ammo for your hunting trips. But you may not have your Bible with you when Satan confronts you, so it's important to memorize Scripture. You don't know which ammo you'll need when. The Bible is a weapon full of ammo (God's truth) to fight temptations.

As I sat up to shoot at that flock of widgeon, before I realized that the birds are too far left for anyone else to get a good shot without shooting across me, I picked out the one bird I had been tracking. Most folks new to duck hunting see a flock of birds and struggle to pick one out. Then they end up shooting at the whole group and often don't hit a thing. After you gain some experience, you learn to focus on a single bird when they're flying around and that's the one you shoot at first.

I had that bird locked in as I brought my gun up. It was almost surreal at that point. I put my bead on the bird, fired, and it fell. After I shot that one, I turned off focus and took in the whole situation. Apparently a group of mallards had come in with the widgeon and now there were birds everywhere. As I found another widgeon and chambered another round in my trusty pump, I squeezed the trigger, and it fell. I don't even remember pumping my third round into the chamber, but I saw the duck climbing to get out of the spread, swung through it, in this case coming up under and through it above, fired, and it fell.

Again, three birds in three shots. And again, in under five seconds. I didn't come up expecting to shoot three birds. I just wanted the one. I didn't know what the birds were going to do. But as I came up, I was ready for anything and being ready paid off. The same thing happened with the huns and pheasants. You don't go into those situations preparing yourself for a triple. And in life, you don't go into situations saying, "Here's when the devil is going to trip me up." But you can be ready for when he's ready to pop out of nowhere with the next temptation.

For Reflection ...

1. How do you prepare for big trips or adventures? Are you a list-maker who packs early to make sure you have everything? Or are you a last-minute person who throws stuff together, hoping you remember everything?

2. Do you tend to plan for the unexpected, or are you more reactionary?

3. What decisions do you need to make about certain temptations before you face them?

4. What's your plan for protecting your heart and mind when facing unexpected temptations? I suggest you start memorizing a few anchor Scriptures that you can refer to when those challenges arise.

5. Practice, practice, practice. And get connected with others who can help hold you accountable and/or help you out when the temptations come. Who can you reach out to today to help you?

9
IT'S A BUCK!

I still remember my first deer. I was twenty-two and a newcomer to archery. But I had friends who had been sportsmen for much longer than I who were able to quickly bring me up to speed. My bow was an older Hoyt that I was given by the parents of my college roommate after he died in a drunk driving accident a year earlier. The bow wasn't fitted for me—the draw length was too long—but the arrows matched well and I made it work. I even became proficient at shooting, practicing from the balcony at our townhome to get used to the elevated angle for tree-stand hunting. I'm not sure the nice elderly lady living below us ever fully appreciated my practicing, but she didn't complain either.

I had spent some time in the woods during the first few weeks of the season, with my friends never far away from me, given my inexperience in deer hunting. I had hunted in this one spot on a National Wildlife Refuge on a Saturday afternoon. We had seen some deer, but I wasn't able to get a shot. The next afternoon, I was back in the same tree. As I recall, I wasn't even in a tree stand—it was more of a platform of branches that I climbed, then pulled my bow up. Before climbing up, I cleared some grass down to the bare ground about fifteen yards out in front of the tree. I poured some doe urine into my "mock scrape," but honestly had no idea what I was doing. It wasn't a good spot for a real scrape, and it's not like I had seen any bucks that I thought I was attracting. But I did it anyway.

It wasn't long before I saw a deer coming out of the woods to my right and heading toward my "scrape." So I got ready! I stood up, rechecked that my arrow was nocked, and got my finger tab positioned on the string. The deer kept coming. I had an either-sex tag, so the fact that it was a doe didn't bother me. Sure enough, it stopped at my scrape and sniffed. That's all I needed. I went to full draw and released the arrow. That arrow hit the mark—a little high, in the spine, and the deer dropped on the spot. Unfortunately when you hit a deer in the spine with an arrow, it usually will require some follow up to dispatch the animal. This one was no different, but I soon had harvested my first deer, with a little help from my knife.

Turned out this doe was a small button buck, or a male fawn. But I had my first whitetail and that first deer came with a bow. I was excited, to say the least. With the help of my more experienced friends, we butchered the deer that night. Staci and I wrapped it up with freezer paper and put it in our freezer the next night.

There may only be one other deer that I'll remember being harvested as clearly as I remember that one—that is, my son's first deer.

In Minnesota, you can't take hunter safety class until you're at least eleven. You need a hunter safety certificate to hunt on your own, and certainly to hunt in other states, as in Michigan, where I regularly go for rifle hunting whitetails. In the spring of 2012, before Rylan turned twelve, we had him go through the hunter safety course. The course was excellent, not only for the coursework, but for the focus on constant safety and the full-day field requirement where the students went through multiple stations learning how to be safe in true-to-life hunting scenarios.

Getting his certificate was a big deal, as it meant he knew how to be safe afield. More importantly, it meant he could get a license when we went to Michigan in the fall. Rylan had spent plenty of days in the double tree stand with me bow hunting. He had participated in a few youth waterfowl hunts, had shot a grouse or two, and had already shot three wild turkeys. So he was no newcomer to hunting. I was determined to start him earlier than I started and get him hooked on the outdoors as young as possible. But taking him deer hunting, with him behind the rifle rather than just watching—this was going to be interesting.

We hunt primarily on private land in Michigan. A former coworker that I now call my friend has allowed me to hunt on his heavily forested land in the Upper Peninsula since 2006. I've been successful each year I've gone up there. I did shoot a small basket rack buck during one hunt, but otherwise I usually take a mature doe for the freezer. We have multiple stand locations that allow us to move around and get variety. We'd enjoy spending evenings with the guys, recapping the day's adventures and planning for the next morning. These conversations are among the most enjoyable things I still do.

Rylan was going to be using my friend's .243 caliber rifle. He hadn't shot a scoped rifle larger than a .22, nor had he seen the property we were hunting before, so we spent a weekend up at the cabin in Michigan in early October.

We visited each of the stands, cleared shooting lanes, built a new stand, giving him an overview of the land we hunt. We let him shoot a few rounds through the .243. All went well and it solidified our excitement for the hunting trip.

We brought the rifle home with us with the plan to get to the range so Rylan could continue getting familiar with the firearm. We spent a couple hours at the local shooting range one Saturday morning. Rylan shot twelve rounds through the rifle, all at fifty yards. Most of our shots in Michigan are at that distance, or less, due to the thick forest. Besides getting him used to the distance we expected to shoot, I figured it would be best to get him confident with his grouping, which was expected to be tighter at that range.

That range trip went well. He wasn't necessarily putting the rounds in a two-inch group, but he was hitting consistently within a six-inch circle, plenty tight enough to harvest a whitetail. Perhaps more importantly, he didn't fear the kick of the rifle. He got used to the safety and the bolt action of the rifle, as well as the scope and target acquisition. We also got the rifle out a couple evenings at home and had him work the bolt, shoulder the gun, and look through the scope, just to continue getting him familiar with the firearm.

In Michigan, the deer hunting season always opens on November 15, regardless of what day of the week it falls on. That year, the fifteenth fell on a Thursday. As a twelve-year-old, Rylan was in seventh grade. The last time I checked, November 15 is not a holiday. That meant pulling Rylan from school for a few days. He knew he had to have his grades up and we were honest in telling the school why he was going to miss school (they approved the absence). We left for Michigan on Tuesday to give ourselves a full day around the camp to settle in, get our gear sprayed down with scent cover-up, and just prepare for opener. We made a last-minute visit to the stand we planned to go to opening morning to clear some leaves out of it and set up our chairs. Then we settled back into camp, had dinner, and made our final plans.

    The alarm went off at 4:15 that morning, and the four of us—Rylan, the host, another friend, and I—had breakfast, a cup of coffee, got dressed, and set off. The morning sit on the stands came and went. The host saw a few deer, but didn't shoot since they passed by fairly early and it was opening morning. We all met back at camp for a quick lunch and nap. Rylan and I didn't nap too long before setting back out for the afternoon. We switched to a new stand location, a bigger stand, overlooking a broad valley of sorts with a great deer trail running down the middle.

    We were there for about an hour or so and were mostly waiting for time to pass. It would be a little closer to dark when we expected deer to start moving. We were chatting quietly about the woods, school, and life in general. There wasn't much wind, so it was a nice quiet afternoon. The sun was starting to peek through the clouds and we were enjoying ourselves.

    It was then that I heard a thump. Rylan said he heard a crash. I knew it was the sound of deer hooves landing on solid ground after jumping over an obstacle. I was struggling with my right ear during the week and couldn't pinpoint where the sound came from. I asked Rylan and he referenced back over our right shoulder. We hadn't seen the deer yet, but I told him to get his rifle up and ready. While he was bringing his gun up, we saw the deer walking.

"It's a buck," Rylan whispered at the same time I saw the antlers. Given that Rylan had both a buck and a doe tag, it didn't matter how big it was. It was walking at a steady pace, mostly quartering away from us. I reached over and flipped the safety off of his rifle, which he now had up and was using the side of our stand as a rest. As the deer kept walking, I softly said, "not yet." Although the deer was in a clear spot, it was facing directly away from us and still walking. The deer turned perpendicular to us and I again whispered, "not yet," because of some trees in the way. The deer took three more steps, right into an opening, a shooting lane we had cleared in October. I made a noise imitating a doe bleat and the buck froze in his tracks. With the deer stopped in a perfect spot, broadside at about fifty yards, I whispered to Rylan, "Now!"

When I eventually gave the okay to shoot, how was this going to go? No reminders to aim right behind the front shoulder. No chance to explain the need to be far enough forward to avoid a gut shot. No reminder to gently squeeze through the trigger. I just had to believe that Rylan was ready. I had confidence he was, because we had prepared.

Preparation for hunting of any kind takes on a myriad of forms. Obviously there's practice with the weapon being used. There simply is no better way to get proficient with any weapon without it. A scoped rifle is no different. There's always a sense of, "If I've looked through one scope, I can hit well through any of them," but in reality it takes time on the setup you'll be hunting with to get good. You need to understand what the rifle recoil feels like so you don't flinch in anticipation of the shot. You need to know the alignment of the reticles and have the eye relief (space between your eye and the scope) down so you can see the reticle without delay or blurring. Of course it is critical to know how to work the safety. You need to understand the action of the rifle, especially for guns like bolt actions, which can all feel a little different. If you need to throw additional rounds at an animal, you don't want to be thinking about how to cycle in the next shell.

Then there's preparing for various situations, or the "What If" game. What if the deer is running? What if it comes in behind us? What if it spots us before we spot it? What if the deer is facing us, broadside, quartering toward or away? What if it's on the other slope or all we see is the head? Over time, experience helps hunters learn the answers to these various questions—but to a new hunter, it's important to have the discussions before encountering them.

For Rylan we worked through the practice part with the rifle. We shot out at the cabin during our early season scouting trip. We went to the range and shot at different distances. We worked through the action at home (unloaded). We looked through the scope regularly. He was ready with the gun.

Then we worked on situational training. We watched hunting programs and noted why they did what they did. I'd stop him on almost any deer picture we saw in his hunting magazines and ask him, "Where would you shoot this one?" When he was sleeping on the bottom bed of his bunk bed, he had actually taped a picture of a deer with the vitals outlined on it on the bottom of the top bunk so he could see it every night as he went to sleep and every morning as he woke up. He was ready!

With that kind of preparation, it all comes down to execution. Putting it all together. One of the main things required at the execution point is focus. All of the mechanics and shot placement thoughts need to be on autopilot. You're not thinking about anything, but your focus is such that you're thinking about everything. Most likely you're focused intently on the animal and what it's doing. That's what you need to be doing because everything else is in response to the animal. If it is looking at you, don't move. If it's running, stop it. If it's stopped, you need to focus on shot placement.

As a bow hunter, I know that shot placement is hypercritical. I know that I need to aim at specific hairs on a deer rather than to aim at the body. Rifle hunting works the same way. You need to lock in on a specific spot on the deer, not just the "front half" or any other general area. To be effective at putting it all together, it requires that level of focus.

Think about what it takes to be effective for God. In my mind, being effective for God means maximizing our God-given purpose. I believe that God put every one of us here for a specific purpose. Once you know that purpose and focus on it, your effectiveness will go off the charts.

During one of my morning devotion times, I was thinking about what my purpose was and how to figure it out. According to Rick Warren's *The Purpose Driven Life*, I'm here for God's pleasure; for God's family; to become like Christ; to serve God; and to undertake a mission. If you haven't read that book, I highly recommend it as a way to find out why you're here. Pastor Warren does a fantastic job of explaining that.

Though that all makes sense, I sometimes still wonder about how do I fit in? Why am I here? I landed on what I consider a simple way to think about it. I call it P+P=P or Proficiency + Passion = Purpose.

Proficiency is simply whatever you're good at. Everybody has something he or she is good at. How do I know? Because the Bible says so. You see, we're all gifted in some way.

First Peter 4:10 says that "Each of you has been blessed with one of God's many wonderful gifts to be used in the service of others. So use your gift well" (CEV). Romans 12:6 explains that "In his grace, God has given us different gifts for doing certain things well" (NLT). Paul told Timothy about his gifts when he stated, "For this reason I remind you to fan into flame the gift of God, which is in you through the laying on of my hands. For the Spirit God gave us does not make us timid, but gives us power, love and self-discipline" (2 Timothy 1:6–7).

First figure out what you're good at. If you want to think about it in terms of ministry, there are plenty of gift assessments online. Go find one and take it.

You can go a long way and do great things by focusing on what you're good at—but you can do much, much more if you're also working in a zone that you're *passionate* about. What sets your heart on fire?

I was having lunch with a friend at work a couple weeks ago and we were talking about our kids' passions. We struggled a little bit as we pondered where they might land, but both of us agreed that we could hunt and fish every day and never get tired of it. If that isn't an example of passion, I don't know what is. Chances are the things you're passionate about are like hunting and fishing are to me—things I enjoy immensely. Guess what? That's where God wants us to be.

In Ecclesiastes 3:22, Solomon wrote, "I have seen that nothing is better than that man should be happy in his activities" (NASB). He also said, "I know that there is nothing better for people than to be happy and to do good while they live. That each of them may eat and drink, and find satisfaction in all their toil—this is the gift of God" (3:12–13). And later, "Even so, I have noticed one thing, at least, that is good. It is good for people to eat, drink, and enjoy their work under the sun during the short life God has given them, and to accept their lot in life. And it is a good thing to receive wealth from God and the good health to enjoy it. To enjoy your work and accept your lot in life—

this is indeed a gift from God. God keeps such people so busy enjoying life that they take no time to brood over the past" (Ecclesiastes 5:18–20, NLT).

Did you get all of that? Be happy in your activities. Enjoy your work. Be busy enjoying life. God wants us to work where we're passionate and where we enjoy ourselves. That maximizes what we can do.

In my simple linear thinking, consider what you're good at and what you enjoy doing—and you will have found your *purpose*. It's that simple. Your purpose is shaped by what God has given you the desire to do. In his letter to the church at Ephesus, Paul wrote, "In him we were also chosen, having been predestined according to the plan of him who works out everything in conformity with the purpose of his will" (Ephesians 1:11). In his letter to the church at Corinth, Paul explained that "The one who plants and the one who waters have one purpose, and they will each be rewarded according to their own labor" (1 Corinthians 3:8).

Take note, though, that the "formula" only really works in reverse. You see, we all have the same purpose: *to actively work to advance God's kingdom*. The details of how each of us do that are different. Remember that your assignment in the kingdom will usually be enjoyable. You should be effective at it because that is how God has gifted you, and He has given you the desire (the passion) to accomplish everything He has in mind for you.

I urge you to spend some time in prayer reflecting on

your passions and where you're proficient—both in the context of your purpose. You can talk to others who know you well for additional guidance. Again, you can take online assessments to find your giftings. Be sure you're listening to God for His guidance. He brought you into this world for something specific and will guide you into that assignment as you diligently seek God's will in this regard.

Once you figure out your specific purpose, that is, your ministry, you need to focus on it so that you are always working in "the zone." We can not only prepare for that but get better at it over time. In 1 Thessalonians 4:1, Paul said, "We instructed you how to live in order to please God, as in fact you are living. Now we ask you and urge you in the Lord Jesus to do this more and more." Later in verse 10 he said, "Yet we urge you, brothers and sisters, to do so more and more." To me, when Paul encourages them to do things "more and more," he's telling them to keep going. To keep doing more of what they do well. To keep practicing. To keep advancing the kingdom through their ministries.

As I whispered the word "Now" to my son, the .243 put out a loud "crack." I had shot two deer with that borrowed .243 rifle before I bought my own .30-06 for deer hunting. One of those deer ran about thirty yards and fell over and died. The other, a smaller deer, I hit farther back and it ran for a hundred yards before expiring. I wasn't sure what was going to happen.

As my son's shot rang out, the deer literally fell over. I saw where he hit—it was a great double lung shot. The .243 isn't a huge rifle, but it did the trick. I told Rylan to cycle the action to have another live round in the chamber. We watched for a few seconds. As the deer was expiring, it was clear he wasn't getting up. I instructed Rylan to put his safety back on. He did so and put the gun back down. I just watched my son shoot his first whitetail deer—a buck no less.

I grabbed my camera and began videotaping him. In the early part of the video, you can still see the deer taking its last breaths in the background. It's not the scene that's exciting, though. It's the twelve-year-old in the stand with me that's so memorable. Watching him cycle through his adrenaline, even to this day, gives me chills. He encourages the deer to "go to sleep," showing compassion for the life he just took. He looks up and says, "Thank you, Lord," giving thanks to God for the whole experience. He replays the story for me, although it just happened and I clearly experienced everything that happened. During his storytelling, he compliments me for stopping the deer—acknowledging that his accomplishment wasn't a one-man show.

I continue to record the walk out to the deer, watch as he pokes it to make sure it's dead, and puts his hands on its antlers for the first time. A nice five-pointer with a huge body. A great first deer. One he'll never forget. Neither will his dad.

For Reflection ...

1. What are you passionate about? I'm not talking about something you like to do, but rather something you could look forward to doing every day.

2. What are you good at? In what areas do you think God has gifted you, in ministry or not? What are your specific talents?

3. Think about the intersection of your passion and your talents. What do you think you should be doing to maximize your strengths while enjoying what you do? Talk with others who are close to you and see what they think. And pray. Ask God where He wants you to focus the limited time we have on earth to make a difference for Him.

10
TACKLE BOX

It's probable that if you ask ten different people about their favorite method to catch the same species of fish, you'll get ten different answers. Same with asking people about where to fish as they look out over a lake. They may each have a different idea on where the fish will be. They may all go out on the lake and catch fish, each in a different spot with a different method. There might be one method or area that produces the most fish that day. The next day, it might be a different method or area.

Each summer our family heads to central Minnesota to a small resort on a medium-sized lake. The resort is called Bear Paw on Lake Washburn and has been around since 1946. Until recently, the cabins looked like they were built in the forties, but that didn't matter to us. We always go the last week of July and four other families always go with us at the same time. We consider that group to be some of our closest friends—even though we only see most of them during that one week each year.

That time of year, we essentially have the resort to ourselves. There are only five cabins up there anyway and we fill them up. The resort has always been a safe place for the kids. Small groups of them can be seen roaming through the resort, or playing in the water, or fishing from the docks or out in the small boats and kayaks. The women tend to spend most of their days on the end of the big dock, soaking up the sun, catching up on books, and otherwise discussing whatever it is that women talk about hanging out all day.

The guys are usually out at dawn fishing, back for a quick nap and bite to eat, then out swimming, waterskiing, pulling the kids around on tubes, sunning ourselves while trying to follow the ladies' conversations, reading magazines in the shade, or fulfilling other relaxation duties.

It's a week we look forward to every year.

For many years, Dan and I would get up around six o'clock, hook up his trailered fourteen-foot Lund to the truck, and head out to Lake 26. More recently, Rylan has been coming with us as well. Most mornings, my alarm goes off a little before six, I sneak into the kids' room and jostle Rylan to make sure he's awake. Then I carefully walk through the soft mat of pine needles around all of the cabins and whisper into the window where Dan is sleeping. Usually there comes a reply back out the window acknowledging that he's awake. Then I know he's up and we'll be meeting at the truck in about ten minutes—depending on how long it takes him to get his Pop-Tart out of the toaster. Back in our cabin I make sure Rylan is up and dressed, grab a cup of coffee and quick bite, then head out the door.

Hooking up the trailer is fast and easy. We make a quick check on the life jackets and see that the needed gear is still in the boat, and we head off. Lake 26 is about twenty minutes from the resort. With the exception of a couple miles right in front of the resort, most of the drive is on a gravel road through the woods. If you've ever been to central Minnesota, or anywhere else with woods for that matter, gravel roads surrounded by woods in the early morning is a perfect place to see deer—in the road—at the last minute. Thankfully we've never had a truck-meets-deer incident.

The launch to Lake 26 is a spot along the road where the shoreline cattails have been removed and there's a sandy lake bottom. The drop-off from the road to the actual lake is only about two feet and not steep at all. The lake bottom in that area is shallow, meaning that we need to push the boat out quite a ways to get it floating. Fortunately, Dan's boat is light enough that we can just get it close to floating and push it off the trailer. The truck tires sometimes make it into the water on low-water years, to close the distance a bit, but we've never struggled to get the boat into or out of the water. We do have to be quick in launching, though, as the bare spot in the cattails happens to be right on an s-curve in the road, where logging trucks often frequent.

Soon after launching and pulling the truck to the side of the road, the trolling motor comes down and we're throwing our favorite lures in pursuit of largemouth bass. Dan knew about this lake from when he was younger, so he would go to the same resort every summer, even working there for a few of them. The lake is a dandy bass fishery that is largely unpressured. There are a few houses around the shoreline, but only a few, and those folks don't seem to be fishing types—which is good for us.

For the longest time, Dan and I would target the bass in the lake using either a lipless crankbait (which is like a hard plastic two-inch "fish" with two sets of treble hooks off the bottom) or a white spinnerbait. That was it. That was enough to keep the action going. There are a couple areas of lily pads on the lake where we'd throw top-water lures imitating frogs to try to entice the bass. There's nothing like the heart-stopping explosion of a bass through the pads—as the fish launches itself up at what it thinks is an easy meal.

We kept things simple in terms of lures because it worked and because I'm not entirely sure that I knew of other methods that we could try.

Once Rylan joined us and brought his bass tournament fishing know-how to bear, that's when we started to try new things. Texas-rigged worms. Swim jigs. Wacky-rigged Senkos. Using those techniques seemed to open the lake up to a whole new set of opportunities. We could now fish in areas we hadn't tried before. Fish that wouldn't bite our aggressive lures would hit the more subtle action of worms. Our fishing success went way up when we started using a wider array of techniques.

Skilled fishing requires targeting a species. Once you know what species you're chasing, you figure out where to find it—what is its habitat and where within a lake are they going to be. On a lake like Lake 26, like most Minnesota lakes in the summertime, it's a safe bet that fish are going to be hanging in the weeds or under the few docks that are there.

After finding them, you need to consider their mood, which is often based on seasonal or weather changes for fish. When we go to Lake 26, it is in the middle of summer.

Fish in an unpressured lake are eating what shows up and, with the warmer water, are willing to chase a little more—most of the time.

When you put together the species, the area and habitat that you're fishing in, and the mood of the fish, you then think about the best approaches—presentations, lures, bait—to get one to bite. Sometimes you have flexibility in those variables, sometimes not. On Lake 26, we have all kinds of flexibility.

Maybe you're on a lake and just want to catch *a* fish. What species might be there and how can I catch it? What if the best method is something you're not prepared for because you brought the wrong tackle? What if the lake you're on doesn't have the species you wanted, but you still want to catch fish? You improvise! I've fished before when the fish weren't hitting what I thought they would, based on species, habitat, and mood. It was frustrating at first. But then I started to think about it and experiment a bit more. Chances are, the reason I was not catching a fish wasn't because they weren't there or didn't want to bite. Instead, it was likely that I wasn't putting something in front of them that they were interested in. On some lakes, they just haven't seen what I'm offering before, and it takes a few casts and tweaks to my fishing style to entice them to bite. I need to have a tackle box with an assortment of ways to catch a fish, so I'm ready for anything.

What if we aren't chasing bass, but like Jesus suggested, fishing for men? Isn't it the same? I'd like to suggest that evangelism, that is making known the message of the gospel or simply sharing the good news, is similar. You know the species: the lost. The habitat: anywhere. Their mood: that depends. The presentation: that's up to you.

To begin, you just need to start fishing. Did you know that less than 10 percent of Christians regularly "share Christ" with others? Some of the common reasons are fear of being rejected or embarrassed; fear of not having answers; it doesn't cross their mind; they don't know what to say; or they haven't found a way to share that fits their personal style.

Those aren't reasons, they're excuses. In Matthew 28:19–20, Jesus said, "Therefore go and make disciples of all nations." He didn't say, "Go, unless you're afraid of being embarrassed." He didn't say, "Go, unless you forget about it." He just said, "Go!" Jesus wanted us to go because people who do not yet know Him are lost, without hope, and are destined for destruction. So while it may be uncomfortable for you, you may be afraid of being rejected, or you may not know what to say, you need to go anyway. We have the answer they're seeking, whether they know they're looking or not—and that answer is Jesus.

So, you understand the need and you're ready to go fishing for men. Now what? Where do you start? Two primary methods. According to 1 Peter 4:11, "If anyone speaks, they should do so as one who speaks the very words of God. If anyone serves, they should do so with the strength God provides, so that in all things God may be praised through Jesus Christ." Did you get that? The two ways we are supposed to show people the path to Jesus are speaking and serving or quite simply: *words* and *works*.

Let's be honest here. Some of you just gave a sigh of relief. I know I did the first time I read that. You know why? Because we all think that works are easier. And I still believe they can be easier—and effective. First Peter says that those trying to reach the lost can do so "without words, by the behavior" (3:1). That means you can get involved. Be the hands and feet of God by serving. Remember, serving can involve more than just showing up—although that's the clear first step. Try to: (1) Stay positive and have a good attitude. (2) Treat people with respect and dignity. (3) Be a blessing to others. (4) Don't compromise your beliefs. (5) Forgive others quickly.

In the end, be an example. Perhaps you've heard of the saying, "You may be the only Jesus people ever see." If that's the case, be an accurate reflection of Jesus. A great challenge in the Bible comes from 1 Corinthians when Paul tells the church to "follow my example, as I follow the example of Christ" (11:1). Earlier in that book, Paul says it even more directly, "Therefore I urge you to imitate me" (4:16). I constantly reflect on my life to see if I am living a life worthy of imitating. Am I being a good example? Do your own reflection by asking the same questions.

There is a thought that being friendly, helpful, and neighborly may be necessary in preparation for evangelism, but it is not a substitute for evangelism. Christianity cannot be simply radiated—the good news must be expressed. You can't just rub shoulders with someone and expect him or her to "catch" the good news. They may see an example of what a relationship with Jesus looks like, but they won't be able to understand it just by watching. That's where our words come in. This is the part that seems hard. Peter encourages us by saying, "Always be prepared to give an answer to everyone who asks you to give the reason for the hope that you have" (1 Peter 3:15). Think about your answer and have it ready. That gets us ready for the times when people ask us about what motivates our good works and gracious interactions with others.

What about when we aren't "caught" doing something good, but instead have the opportunity to actually talk to someone instead? The message we need to get across is that we were all good with God back in the Garden of Eden, but the serpent (Satan) brought sin into the world and that separated us from God. God provided a bridge back to Him as a means to overcome the sin that still separates us—that bridge is Jesus. Jesus took our sin—yours and mine—with Him to the cross. According to Romans 10:9, "If you declare with your mouth, 'Jesus is Lord,' and believe in your heart that God raised him from the dead, you will be saved."

That's the message. But how to share it? This is where you need to find the right lure, and the right presentation, to "catch the fish." The presentation is going to be based on where they are in their journey.

For instance, some folks may be seeking. They may know something is missing and have heard that there's a better way. Perhaps someone else's actions planted the seed, but you're the one who gets to talk to them. The approach with that person could be fairly direct.

How about the stranger next to you on the airplane? Maybe after they ask you what you're reading (a Christian book perhaps) or listening to (maybe a Christian song), you could say something like, "Do you think there is a heaven and hell?" And if they say yes, you can follow with "Which one do you think you'll go to?" Regardless of their answer, follow with a "Why?" The answer to that question will guide the rest of the conversation. If they talk about going to hell because they've done bad things, you need to explain how someone has already paid for those "bad" things and tell them how they can accept that payment for themselves (see Romans 10). If they talk about going to heaven because "basically I'm a good person" then you can follow with a discussion about how you can never be good enough to reach God's standard of perfect righteousness.

The point is that you can find the "aggressive" fish or the "content" fish and need to have enough lures and know-how to present them to catch either one. There are many resources available to help you learn more techniques, conversation starters, and other methods to engage people and lead them to Jesus. (Consider reading *Nudge* by Leonard Sweet or *Questioning Evangelism* by Randy Newman.) Investigate them and find your favorites. By doing so, you can get a set of options that you're comfortable with and overcome the fears we spoke about earlier.

Let me add a note of caution here. There are three significant risks involved with evangelizing. The first, with people who know you well, is the danger that the way you live may not be in sync with the message you try to share with them. If you're cheating on your timesheet, lying to your spouse, swearing at the driver in front of you, or rude to your dinner server—and then try to evangelize a coworker or family member who saw all of that—there are going to be problems. You may get them to accept Jesus, but they won't have an idea of what to do next. The example you've given isn't one that matches the love that you explained Jesus offers. You need to have the credibility to share the message effectively. Remember, be worthy to imitate.

A second risk is that you can dilute the message. Maybe you're so anxious to get someone to say yes to Jesus that you soften the message. You see, one of the main parts of someone accepting the gospel and turning to Jesus is that they need to repent of his or her sins. That means they will need to change some things in their life, sometimes significant things. They may need to change their lifestyle, separate from old friends, spend their time and money differently, get rid of things in their house, and so on and so on. The message of Jesus' redemptive death on the cross needs to include a change in a person's heart. There needs to be a more tangible change in their life as well. Getting one without the other is not a full acceptance of Jesus' sacrifice. I'm not saying you can't simplify the message or get creative in your presentation. Pick a method with which you feel comfortable. But don't water down God's message of repentance and redemption.

Finally, there is a risk that after the first time you talk to someone and they accept Jesus, you'll develop an addiction of your own—an addiction to evangelizing. You'll want to tell everyone you see about Jesus—the postman, your student's teacher, the grocery store cashier, your friends and family. No one will be safe from you spreading the gospel. This is one addiction of which the Lord approves.

When I reflect on this last year of fishing on Lake 26, I remember using all sorts of techniques while we were chasing bass. I remember catching some of the biggest fish we've caught. Several four-pound and a five-pound fish. None of those came on the lures or presentations that Dan and I used to catch fish on. We changed it up and found a whole new way to be successful on the water. The wacky-rigged Senko became a go-to presentation that landed all four of the biggest fish. With those different techniques still in my tackle box, I can't wait to get back out there and try some more.

Go fishing! Develop your own favorite approach. Be comfortable with it. But also have others at the ready. The better prepared your "tackle box," the better prepared you'll be to "catch fish." Maybe you'll get addicted to Christ's admonition to go fishing for men (see Matthew 4:19).

For Reflection ...

1. Write out your faith journey/testimony on a 3x5 note card. Try to fit it on the card, which will force you to keep it brief. Then memorize it and say it out loud to somebody. It never hurts to know clearly and succinctly what Jesus has done for you personally.

2. How good are you when it comes to improvising? Are you more of a planner, or more of a go-with-the-flow type of person?

3. Which non-Christian in your circle of relationships is most likely to be receptive to the gospel? How could you most effectively present the good news of Christ to this person in a way that's meaningful to him or her?

4. Add more tools to the toolbox. What other conversation starters can you have in mind? Where else throughout your regular weekly routine do you encounter people who do not yet have a personal relationship with Jesus as their Lord and Savior? Constantly refresh your list and keep adding tools.

5. Celebrate with friends after such conversations. Heaven rejoices when people accept Jesus and God smiles at you when you are His vessel to reach them.

11
OFF ROAD

Now it's no secret that I like to hunt and fish and enjoy other outdoor activities. In order to do many of those things, it is useful to have a truck. The truck is good for pulling, transporting, and getting to locations where I can enjoy the outdoors. The truck is necessary to pull our boat. Our Sportfish isn't a huge boat, but a car isn't going to pull it around, especially on the hilly roads of Canada. The truck also allows me to carry all of my hunting gear and two Labrador Retrievers when I go on bird hunting trips. Although folks do put their deer on their hoods or on storage racks behind their vehicles, the bed of the truck is a great place for transporting harvested game.

There's the usefulness of the truck to just get around. Sure, gas mileage is better in a car when going long distances, but what about when you get there? Doing the things I like to do doesn't mean we can always stick to paved roads and parking lots. Many times when we've been duck hunting, we've driven out into a cut corn field to set up and take down decoys. A car wouldn't survive that many times. The roads we're typically on during our bird hunting trips to North Dakota are more often made of gravel rather than pavement. No question, cars can do just fine on gravel roads, but when the roads are "minimum maintenance"—the official designation for dirt roads in certain parts of the country—things can get a little hairy.

Dan and I were driving around the roads of south central North Dakota, spending plenty of time on gravel. We were scouting for ducks using fields and also watching ditches for pheasants that were coming to the roads for the gravel but may have been spooked by the oncoming truck. We've often been with friends who are out doing the same thing, as we try to find a place to chase ducks and geese the next day. However, Dan and I are usually looking more down than up, knowing those guys are better at finding good duck fields anyway.

We've gotten familiar with the roads in the area we hunt and know where we can and can't go when the roads are wet. Thankfully, we never learned that the hard way. We're careful about avoiding the spots that might get us in trouble. I remember when we turned off one gravel road onto a minimum maintenance road. It was more like a two-track road used by a farmer to access his field. But it seemed like we weren't the first to want to use it and it saved us several miles. That road was going to get us closer to a spot we wanted to be via a more direct route.

As we started down the road, there was a slight incline, just enough to block our view of the entire thoroughfare. As we crested the small incline, we noted a wetland waiting for us at the bottom. If our only option had been to go through the wetland, which had standing water, we would've turned around. However, the many vehicles that had taken this path before us had all veered left around the flooded wetland to get back on track on the other side. It hadn't rained during that trip, so we figured the little detour the others had taken would be good enough.

As we were rolling up to the detour, I switched the truck into four-wheel drive. All it took was the turn of a knob. I wasn't even sure I'd need it—it looked like solid ground to me.

As I veered off the main road onto the detour around the wetland, I was instantly glad I was in four-wheel drive. I could tell we were sinking a bit and all of the tires were struggling to gain traction. As the truck slowed, bogging down in the mud, I gave it more gas. I'd power through the mud, get up on top of the deep stuff, stay there by going faster, and we'd be fine. Just as I gave it gas, it happened. My truck, equipped with automatic traction control, thought it was smarter than me.

The traction control senses when a wheel is spinning and shifts power from that wheel to another, hoping to find one that is gripping. For those unfamiliar with this feature, picture a car or truck turning a corner on slick roads. We have plenty of those in Minnesota. Winter tends to bring out the young man in most guys who are just too tempted by the possibility of a little controlled fishtail. You can do this by hitting the gas a bit when going through a turn. As you go through the turn and hit the gas, the traction control senses that the rear wheels are spinning and pulls the power from them until the vehicle is lined back up. That's a great feature—unless you're actually trying to get the wheels to spin. You can turn off the traction control, though it's not recommended.

So, here we were on the muddy detour route and I'm ready to get the most out of having all four wheels spinning to get me through this. But the harder I push on the gas, the less power I have. I'm pushing on the gas because I need the juice, not because I want to see how much I can be robbed of power in the truck. This didn't feel like it was going to turn out well.

That was in full-time four-wheel drive. My truck also has the ability to go into "automatic" four-wheel drive. This is the feature in which the truck decides when having all of the wheels powered is necessary, but also just limits it to the two rear tires when it isn't necessary. Seems like it should result in greater fuel efficiency since powering all four wheels all of the time takes a little extra oomph.

During a recent trip to visit Dan's family, he and I were able to sneak away a few times over several days to get out for the last of the Minnesota grouse season and do some ice fishing. During the first few days of our visit, it was snowing almost constantly. Not hard, but enough to keep a fine layer of the slick stuff on roads. In many places, we could still see the pavement, but there were plenty of extended spots where the roads were covered with snow. I wasn't sure how well the truck was tracking on these roads, so I went with the "automatic" four-wheel drive option. We'd probably be okay with just two-wheel drive and the rear wheels powered, but if we hit spots that were a bit more slippery, the truck could step in for me and send some additional power to the front tires and keep us on the road.

It worked like a charm. We never were worried about sliding off the road, and we safely traveled to where we were going.

Isn't life like those roads at Dan's over the winter? Oftentimes, we can move through life in two-wheel drive, and that works. Our lives are manageable and we can rely on a minimum amount of "power" to keep us going forward. We can go to church on Sunday and pray before meals and feel like we're aptly powered. Maybe we'll give a friend a hand when he moves, or carry an elderly person's grocery bag to their car. Just like our truck on dry roads, that doesn't require anything special in terms of power to the wheels or power distribution. We can do that on our own.

But what about when we hit a difficult time in life? We lose our job or a loved one to death. We struggle in our marriages. We realize we aren't talking with our kids anymore. We consistently spend more than we make. We can't break our addiction to drugs, alcohol, or pornography. Then what?

During those times is when many guys will turn to prayer and seek out Jesus. And it helps if they have friends who will intercede or intervene or just get intertwined with their troubled life. Those friends come through like putting the truck in full-time four-wheel drive, and it helps us get through slippery and muddy areas. It's great to know that such a setting exists—that a deeper level of power exists.

Many a Christian success story comes from those situations where someone got too deep in trouble and had a "come-to-Jesus" moment when they realized their deepest needs could only be met by a reconciled relationship with God through Jesus. I've heard plenty salvation stories over the years and they still give me chills.

To know God is working among us now continues to give me hope for those who don't yet know.

What about the "automatic setting" for life? I must admit, most of my spiritual life is spent in two-wheel drive. Overall, I have a low-risk life. That may be true of you too. We don't spend countless hours on the front lines, taking the gospel to those who haven't heard it. We don't use our spare time working with homeless or poor or disadvantaged people. We defer to others who have that "calling" and assume they're handling the needs.

The problem with spending so much time in two-wheel drive is that we often get lulled into kind of a road daze when we may not be able to see the muddy areas coming anymore. Before we know it, we're trying to push the gas pedal, waiting for all four wheels to get power, but we didn't switch to four-wheel drive. Then we're stuck. We joke with the guys about the hot new employee, and without thinking about it, take an extra look at her each time we see her. We go to another happy hour with that same group of guys from work—for the fifth time this month. One of the guys invites the new girl and you do some "harmless" flirting. Then you find yourself being the one to invite her to the next happy hour. It's just the work crew, right? Only a few beers. Nothing is going to happen. Except too many times, something does happen. Maybe not even directly with the new girl but maybe just the lack of time with your family at home that starts to cause ripples. Or perhaps worse.

Wouldn't it be better if we were always in the automatic four-wheel drive mode? Sure, most of life is still spent in two-wheel drive, where you can be most efficient. But when life gets slippery, without even knowing it, you drop into four-wheel drive. The guys joke about the hot new girl and your four-wheel drive kicks in and you say how great your wife still looks to you. The next time you see her, you think about your wife at home and look forward to getting home to her. The guys invite you to happy hour, and maybe you go, maybe you don't; but if you go, the whole time you're there, you're in four-wheel drive, in a greater mode of traction to help avoid slippery roads.

In the book of Jeremiah, God shares this with Jeremiah:

> Blessed is the one who trusts in the Lord,
>   whose confidence is in him.
> They will be like a tree planted by the water
>   that sends out its roots by the stream.
> It does not fear when heat comes;
>   its leaves are always green.
> It has no worries in a year of drought
>   and never fails to bear fruit (Jeremiah 17:7–8).

To me, that verse sounds a lot like automatic four-wheel drive. The tree has roots into the water and when heat and drought come, it is unaffected. The "water" we need to put our roots into is God. When we do so, when we have a constant source of "water" to operate in automatic four-wheel drive during times of "drought"—trials, tribulations, temptations, tests—these will not shake us.

How do you get there? *How do we become a "stream tree"?* We weren't born with automatic four-wheel drive. Perhaps we weren't born with our roots by the stream. But it is something we can add to our current way of thinking.

To develop the ability to spend life in automatic four-wheel drive takes a few intentional steps. This isn't just tweaking a minor component, like going on a diet to drop from three sodas each day to just two. This isn't just saying that I need to exercise more. This isn't committing to volunteer once a month at a homeless shelter. This is a major overhaul and requires a significant system add-on. This requires a commitment to change your way of thinking and involves more preparation than running a marathon or climbing Mount Everest. This is not just a one-time period of focus. This is a lifetime decision and requires a lifetime of preparation and maintenance. Just like four-wheel drive in my truck won't work when I need it if I don't make sure the transfer case is lubricated and the right fluids are in there.

Like maintaining the off-road functions of your truck, having a life focused on God takes regular investments in your life—such as daily Bible reading and prayer, sharing in fellowship with other believers, serving at your church and in your community, and being ready to be used by God. For you to maximize your life, to enjoy a life in four-wheel drive, you first need to make the intentional step of acknowledging that you need Jesus.

Would I trust the automatic setting in an area where things were more obviously slippery or muddy or difficult in general? Probably not. It's nice to know that full-time four-wheel drive is at my fingertips in those instances to help ensure the truck can power through them. Same with life. You can make the adjustments in your life to get where your automatic setting is good and you're living life without even thinking about it—even when you're powering through a tough spot. But there are still going to be times when major trials come and you need to have full-time four-wheel drive ready. Those same steps I mentioned above that you need to maintain your system also can prepare your full-time operating system.

That muddy detour around the wetland along the minimum maintenance road in North Dakota was when full-time four-wheel drive was needed. It was an area where the truck was struggling. But we saw it coming and could prepare accordingly. It worked. Although the truck seemed to be robbing the wheels of power when I thought I needed it most, it came through. It set the power distribution at the right level and we cruised right through. Back on the road on the other side of the wetland, I remember looking at Dan and saying that next time I would turn off the traction control before hitting an area like that. Despite the fact that it got us through, it still wasn't the way I wanted it to go.

Are we like that in life too? We keep thinking that we know better. I can go into a situation that might be dangerous or tempting, but I can handle it because I read the Bible this morning. Or because I related to the message at church on Sunday. Or because we grew up in the church.

The better way to go about life, even with your four-wheel drive system fully functional, is to avoid certain situations all the way. When roads are icy, I could say to myself that my truck has four-wheel drive and so I'm good driving around. Ice doesn't care if two wheels are spinning or four—it's not going to give any traction. The best way to be "safe" during those times is to avoid driving unless you absolutely have to. Why put yourself in situations where you know you'll need four-wheel drive? What if it doesn't work? Whatever your temptation may be, avoiding the temptation may still be the best way to ensure success. Rather than running through life with your four-wheel drive always engaged, save it for when you need it, especially in those times when temptations come unexpectedly.

The other time to use your four-wheel drive is for fulfilling your purpose. Remember in the introduction when I gave the example of staying in the middle of the road? To me that illustrated staying in the center of God's will for my life. When I'm there and things are going smoothly, my life is aligned with where God wants me to be. That holds true most of the time, but not always. God will sometimes put obstacles in the middle of the road that push us off to the side or into the ditch.

I'm not saying that God wants our lives to be bumpy all the time. But I do believe that God wants us working outside our comfort zone and may push us out there regularly. You see, when our lives are always smooth, we begin to develop a sense that we're in control. We can keep the car in the middle of the road. However, what we need to remember is that we can't do anything without God. As soon as we think we're the ones keeping the car on the road, God may push us off to deepen our dependence on Him.

God may also push us off the road because He

wants us to do more. When I was arguing with God about starting an organization that linked the outdoors with Christianity, I was trying to keep my wheels in the middle of the road. I was comfortable with where things were in my life and in my relationship with Jesus. But God let me know that He wanted more from me. He didn't want me in the middle of a paved road. He wanted me driving through the field for a while, out where it was bumpy, out where I needed four-wheel drive, out where I needed Him. He knew that would make a bigger difference for Him. He also knew that it would draw me closer to Him. Those two areas are exactly where He wants us—making a difference for Him and continually drawing closer to Him.

Most of the time, keeping your wheels on the road and even in the center of the road where the ride is most smooth may be where God wants us. Living in automatic four-wheel drive allows you to stay there in times of trials and temptations. Having full-time four-wheel drive is useful when challenges come and can help you stay on the road. But having full-time four-wheel drive can also be useful when God provides an opportunity or a positive challenge to get off the road. We need to always be watching for those opportunities to make a difference for Him, to get off the road and explore a little. If you've walked through the steps I've discussed up to this point, your four-wheel drive will be ready to go.

So go on. Be ready for trials. Enjoy life. Practice your faith. Live for God. Put your life in four-wheel drive. Become a stream tree!

For Reflection ...

1. How prepared are you for what God puts in your path, for opportunities and temptations? Is your four-wheel drive ready? How can your four-wheel drive adapt for you when it comes to facing the different challenges in life?

2. Has God ever steered you off the road or made your life bumpy to force you to use four-wheel drive? How did you respond?

3. What do you need to do to become a "stream tree"? Do you need to transplant yourself to a different situation (church, job, friend group) to be closer to a stream? Do you need to grow your roots deeper (read the Bible, join a small group, pray more) to reach the stream?